It is a gift to encounter someone whos blend of inspiration and unwavering support, someone who embodies the very qualities that we all strive to cultivate in our own lives. Eric is one of those exceptional individuals—an example of integrity, purpose, and leadership in every sense of the word. His values, his unwavering purpose, and his desire to make a meaningful difference in the lives of others are examples of his commitment to living with purpose and helping others do the same.

I hope his book serves as both a source of inspiration and a guide for anyone looking to lead with heart, build with intention, and live a life of true meaning. It has been an honor and a privilege call Eric my friend.

—WADE WILDE, CFO, MSSG

No hesitation—I am blessed to have Eric as a friend and colleague. He is a person of high integrity, generosity, professionalism, and faith. I am blessed to call him FRIEND and to endorse his book *What's Your Mindset?*

—DAVID ELLIOTT, President and CEO,
Santa Ana Chamber, Passkeys Foundation

Eric is the kind of leader who lifts others up, follows through on his word, and leads with purpose. I'm proud to call him a colleague and even prouder to support him.

—KEVIN CHOW, President and CEO, Triple S

Eric Goodman is a wonderful father, friend, entrepreneur and philanthropist. He leads a purpose-driven life with energy and passion to ensure those who need his services or philanthropic support have what they need to thrive. I have been impressed by Eric's thoughtfulness and strategy to leverage his vast network of companies and nonprofit organizations in benefit of our community. In his new book, Eric provides real life stories about the positive mindset required to move from good to great, both at work and in life.

—DAWN S. REESE, CFRE, Chief Executive Officer, The Wooden Floor

Eric Goodman is a man grounded in a deep, unshakable faith in a God of rich abundance who reminds us that through Him, all things are possible (see Matthew 19:29). That faith is not just something Eric talks about; it's something he lives every single day. Eric has long believed that the more people he meets, the more people he can help.

That simple but powerful philosophy has shaped his life and his leadership. It's a form of servant leadership that doesn't just inspire, it transforms. It calls us to seek our better angels and to show up for others in meaningful, lasting ways. I hope this book is a way to know and help even more people.

I hold a belief that there's a sacred gift in finding gratitude within our grief, when something that once felt like it happened *to* us becomes something that happened *for* us. Eric embodies this mindset. He lives it, teaches it, and leads with it.

Eric shares more than a message—he shares a lifestyle. And I know my life is better because Eric Goodman is in it.

—DAVID BLAIR, Sr. Director of Philanthropy
Boys and Girls Club of Central Orange Coast

I love this book! In *What's Your Mindset? Meditations on Life and Leadership*, Eric Goodman has crafted a wonderfully balanced collection of real-life stories that resonate deeply with the complexities of struggle, triumph, redemption, and everything in between. (Oh, the places he's been and the things he has done!) Eric's openness and honesty regarding his life help create a true vulnerability that feels so relatable, which for me, is essential for works like this. Personally, I find it rare to encounter this kind of depth in storytelling, which makes it such a refreshing reading experience. In particular, Eric's combination of faith, positivity, dedication to family, friends, and staunch work ethic reverberate throughout, inviting readers, page by page, to reflect on their own journeys. Well done, Eric.

—CHRIS EPTING, Award-winning journalist
and author of more than fifty books,
including numerous bestsellers

I've had the pleasure of working alongside Eric Goodman and can confidently say he is one of the most dedicated and positively engaged leaders I've encountered. Eric brings an infectious energy to every conversation and interaction, matched only by his unwavering follow-through. When Eric says he's going to do something, he does it—with excellence, integrity, and heart.

What truly sets Eric apart is his welcoming attitude and deep-rooted commitment to giving back. Whether it's mentoring others, supporting his community, or simply being present for those around him, Eric embodies a philanthropic mindset that inspires everyone he meets. His leadership is not just about business success—it's about making a meaningful difference.

I have worked with Eric Goodman in a number of capacities and have also had an opportunity to observe him away from "work" when no one is watching. What I love about Eric is that he is consistent and that he focuses on what matters. He has an ability to parse away clutter and hone in on the things that make a difference, all while maintaining steadfast commitment to a set of guiding principles, that make him who he is.

He is a dedicated, detail oriented, and forward-looking chief executive and board member, ever mindful of the fact that we do what we do for others, and in that, he is not only a great leader but a great human being as well and a great friend.

—PHILLIP KANE, CEO, Turbo Tires, Inc.,
Board Member American Heart Association

Eric Goodman is highly committed to his nonprofit activities, and I had the genuine pleasure of working with him when he served as president of the Inland Empire Ronald McDonald House Board. A dedicated, committed leader, Eric enjoys bringing people together to support causes important to him.

He provided tremendous leadership to the Ronald McDonald House, gave generously of his time and talent, was a supportive partner to the houses executive director, and was remarkable in his efforts to engage the entire community in the program.

—NICOLE RUBIN, Board Member and Senior Advisor,
Ronald McDonald House Charities

Eric Goodman is living proof that from pain can come purpose and joy. His story isn't just powerfu; it's transformational. With raw honesty and contagious optimism, Eric challenges us to shift our mindset, reminding us that kindness, resilience, and happiness are choices we get to make every single day. Eric is a living testament to what it means to lift others. His life and journey move people and now, through the pages of *What's Your Mindset?*, his purpose will awaken something in you too. I'm grateful to call him a friend and even more grateful that the world now gets to hear his voice and be inspired by his light.

—BURGANDIE ONEKEA,
Chief Regional Officer, Junior Achievement
of Orange County and Inland Empire

Eric Goodman paves the way for a more human face of leadership—one that normalizes disability, centers on empathy, and creates space for all to thrive. Goodman's influence extends far beyond his own organization, empowering the greater community through his philanthropic vision and the missions of the organizations he uplifts. Eric leads with clarity, humility, and quiet integrity that redefines and reshapes the way we live, work, and connect.

—ANNE TAMMEL, PCC, Founder and CEO,
Poets and Dreamers, LLC, OC CEO Collective

Eric Goodman has truly an inspiring story. But not only is his story inspiring, but so is he. A true leader for others!

—DR STEFAN BEAN, Superintendent,
Orange County Dept. of Education

Eric embodies the values he shares, treats everyone with kindness, and is always willing to help others find their way. He's been a mentor to many—including me—and I'm honored to call him a friend. His story is not only compelling—it's a testament to the power of purpose, resilience, and grace. Through his writing, Eric invites us into a life shaped by conviction and the courage to lead with heart. He inspires not just with words, but through the way he lives. This book is a reflection of that spirit, and it's one I'm proud to recommend.

—CORI VERNAM, Director of Cause,
Antis Roofing & Waterproofing

Eric has a radiant smile, and day after day, wherever he goes, he lights up the rooms. I remember the day Eric called me and asked if I would be his mentor. I was taken aback. He told me the story behind his smile, how his journey was no fairy tale. Yet through all the hardships, he chose to see the bright side and to "be happy," no matter what occurred. That's when it hit me! I realized that positivity is not a lucky charm—it's "a choice." I'm proud to be Eric's friend, his story will uplift and inspire you just like he has me.

—CHARLES ANTIS, Founder and CEO,
Antis Roofing & Waterproofing

What's Your Mindset?

Meditations on Life and Leadership

Eric L. Goodman

Published by Goodman Publishing
www.ericgoodman.org

ISBN: 979-8-9997378-0-9 (softcover)
ISBN: 979-8-9997378-1-6 (hardcover)
ISBN: 979-8-9997378-2-3(ebook)

Cover design: Eric Goodman, Grant Goodman, and Robby Saligman
Editing and interior design: Creative Editorial Solutions

Special thanks to Chris Epting for helping shape and refine my ideas throughout this writing journey.

Printed in the United States of America
First printing, August 2025

For additional resources, speaking engagements, or more information, visit: www.ericgoodman.org

Dedication

To my family—your love, patience, and belief in me have been my greatest encouragement.

To my mentors and friends—thank you for your wisdom, honesty, and the countless conversations that shaped my thinking.

To everyone who has ever struggled with disabilities, self-doubt, faced adversity, or questioned their path—this book is for you. May *What's Your Mindset?* remind you that growth is always possible, purpose is always within reach, and the way you think can change your life.

To LifeMastery: I now practice Mind, Body, Soul and Spirit. From success to significance. The most powerful person in the room has God with them. Love God, Love people and bring disciples. I am doing kingdom building every day through my life, family, and work. Everything in life is about your mindset. From pain comes purpose.

CONTENTS

FOREWORD

The first time I truly felt the impact of Eric's presence was at the Ronald McDonald House board retreat in Los Angeles, where all the boards of the Southern California homes gathered. I was overwhelmed with fear, knowing we were about to double the size of the Orange County house. As the outspoken member on the board, I felt the weight of expectation from the doctors and business owners around me. It was a daunting task, one I sensed I was called to take on, almost like a divine mission.

Yet I hesitated until that retreat, where I encountered a genuinely kind man whose positive energy was palpable. Eric shared his own ambitious goal of raising $12 million, and in that moment, he became the bridge to my "maybe." Hearing him articulate his vision sparked a flicker of hope within me: Maybe I could do it too. Just knowing he was there, having walked a similar path, empowered me to say yes when the time came to lead the capital campaign. It's ironic that Eric sees me as his mentor, when, in reality, it was his light that shone brightly on a hill for me and all the families at the Orange County house.

Eric is someone who connected with me early on, recognizing my journey and the story I had to share. He approached me for help, and I was more than willing to assist. However, I was also a bit scared by his diligence. He was fully committed to everything I advised him to do, mirroring my own strategies and approaches. His dedication was so intense that I felt the weight of responsibility; if I was wrong, it could hurt him.

One thing I emphasize in life is the power of "maybe." In my previous book, I talked about shifting my mindset from "no" to "yes." I go to sleep with the possibility of "maybe," and that's when miracles happen. Eric embodies this "yes" mentality. He took my advice on storytelling seriously, even hiring my storytelling coach, Jay Golden, and as a result, his narrative has flourished. Initially, I felt he wasn't sharing the entirety of his story, but he has become authentically himself in a profound way.

What's especially noteworthy is how Eric took my concept of fearless giving and made it work. Initially, he was nervous about whether this model could truly succeed, but he fully embraced the principles I shared as a mentor. By committing wholeheartedly to the process, he proved that my model not only works but can lead to tangible success. This validation serves as a beacon of hope for others, demonstrating that with courage and dedication, anyone can achieve their dreams and make a meaningful impact.

Eric has transformed into a significant brand, winning awards and gaining recognition. We're even starting a company together. The power of our stories will be at the forefront when we launch. His reputation in the community is stellar, and his vulnerability is truly inspiring.

Eric's journey is remarkable. He has powerful stories filled with goodness, and it's incredible to witness his evolution. He is fully committed. He is willing to invest in his mission, engaging with boards and communities, and dedicating resources to philanthropy, all while operating on much thinner margins than many businesses.

Both Eric and I prioritize self-care, albeit in different ways. He draws strength from his faith, while I find balance through nature and meditation. Eric is genuinely a pure soul; his energy is palpable when he enters a room. People can sense his positive intentions, which makes a significant impact.

It's vital for Eric to share his stories. At this point in his life, he's laying down his experiences and insights so others can emulate them. His approach shows that giving back isn't a sacrifice; it strengthens culture and community. Eric's ability to connect with people is remarkable, and it reflects in his business success. He proves that anyone, regardless of their industry, can give fearlessly and see the rewards—not just in terms of personal fulfillment but also in business growth.

Eric's goodness is authentic and resonates deeply. He inspires those around him, including me. Our backgrounds may differ, but we share a common belief in the importance of giving and community. Eric truly embodies the spirit of sharing love, food, and shelter.

He's the kind of person who, once he breaks free from any constraints, soars to incredible heights. His presence uplifts the entire community. He's quietly confident—unlike others who seek the spotlight for its own sake. Eric is proud of his contributions and remains humble, a rare combination that sets him apart.

In essence, Eric is a beacon of goodness, inspiring others to follow his lead. He shows that anyone can make a difference, and I'm grateful to have him by my side on this journey.

—Charles Antis
Founder of the Antis Foundation

INTRODUCTION

When I was a child, I was diagnosed with Scheuermann's kyphosis, which is a rare skeletal disorder that causes the vertebrae to grow unevenly. Most people have heard of scoliosis because they would check kids for it in elementary school. That's how I found out I had the disease. Scheuermann's is similar but much more severe; scoliosis might be a 45-degree curvature, while Scheuermann's can be a 90-degree curvature. At its most severe, one is hunched over.

I knew I was eventually going to have surgery for my condition but doctors don't want to do surgery too early in life because it stunts your growth. My parents and I went to Children's Hospital in Los Angeles to see a special orthopedic surgeon who ran tests and referred us to Loma Linda Children's Hospital which was close to where we lived. There I was scheduled for surgery. My condition was putting pressure on my internal organs and my lungs were collapsing, so without surgery, I was not expected to live. This news was devastating to me, my parents, and my family.

I was fifteen and a half years old when my life changed forever. I had a nine-hour operation that included opening my entire back from the top of my neck to the bottom of my back, exposing my entire spine, and then inserting metal rods connected from my shoulder to my hips. Portions of my rib bones were fused with my spine to support my body. I spent eleven days in ICU, thirty-one days total in the hospital, and nine months in a full-body cast.

Because my spine was straightened, I grew two inches on the operating table!

My parents put their lives on hold to care for me. My dad, who owned his own company, would come to the hospital every morning and stay with me until my mom arrived.

The cast was molded from my body, similar to one used for a broken arm or leg. This cast was then cut in half with large metal clips on the side to open and close it. I had to wear the cast when I was standing, but I could take it off at night in bed. Once it was off, though, I could not move anything but my head. I had to depend on my family to help me. I couldn't reach for anything or move for any reason. I would lie in my bed and look out the window at the mountains and dream about life after I was healed. The cast was heavy, and it was summertime. It itched and was hot.

I had to have physical therapy to get my strength back. I was in ninth grade when I had surgery and in tenth grade when I went back to school. In the interim, I was homeschooled while doing therapy. Most of the year before, during, and after my surgery I can't remember. I honestly think I had PTSD from the entire experience. My friends talked about my cast and condition. I don't remember any particular bullies, but there were mean kids who said mean things. It was a horrible and traumatic situation for a teenager to be in while all my friends were out having fun and enjoying the summer together. Having this and other disabilities for more than fifteen years before the surgery was hard.

By the time I was seventeen, life was close to normal. I

couldn't touch my toes, and I couldn't lift anything over ten pounds (I still can't). But because of the sacrifices of my family and the skill of the doctors, I was getting back to myself.

Retelling this story now, more than thirty years later, I believe that what happened to me set the stage for the rest of my life. I have learned two things. First, this experience gave me empathy toward others with disabilities who can't take care of themselves and depend on others and gave me compassion to help those in need.

Second, I have devoted my life ever since to helping others with disabilities. My business, MVS, Inc., has been servicing homes for developmentally disabled adults and children with food and medical supplies for more thirty-eight years. We service more than five hundred homes today. And for more than twenty-three years, I've been on the Board of Directors for Ronald McDonald House Charities, helping parents to be present for their kids who are hospitalized—just like I was.

This book shares my approach in creating positive change through a positive mindset. It's written to provide inspiration for leaders like you—whether you're a well-established leader or are ready to step to the next level of your journey—to turn and face the world with all of your gifts.

The book is designed as a journey through the rhythms of my life, which I've divided into stories (chapters). Within each chapter, you'll find a collection of short, straightforward stories that capture moments of inspiration and reflection. Whether you choose to read this book from start to finish or open it at random, my hope is that you discover something meaningful on each page. Through it all, I've learned a powerful truth: You can change your life by changing your mindset. Each chapter will share a piece of my life, filled with moments of faith, love, leadership and purpose. After each story, I'll highlight a few key lessons that really drive home the message so you can walk away with some practical takeaways. My hope is that these insights inspire you to embrace your own journey and see just how much your mindset can shape your reality.

A View of the Mountains

I was born in San Bernardino, California—a name you might recognize as the birthplace of McDonald's. Yes, that's right, the fast-food giant that changed the way we eat was born here, amid the palm trees and sun-soaked streets. If you want the real scoop on McDonald's, I highly recommend watching *The Founder*, featuring Michael Keaton. The film narrates the story of the McDonald brothers and their humble beginnings in San Bernardino. It chronicles their triumphs and the struggles they faced in trying to create a successful franchise model. Then enters Ray Kroc, who visited their quaint little restaurant and claimed the title of "founder," fabricating the narrative that McDonald's had its roots in Chicago. A twist of fate that forever altered the course of fast-food history.

San Bernardino holds a special place in my heart, and *The Founder* is one of my favorite films—right after *Forrest Gump*, of course. It's more than just entertainment; it's a rich tapestry of my hometown's history and a treasure trove of business lessons on success, ethics, and values. I've watched it countless times, each viewing revealing a new layer of insight that I carry with me to this day. Kroc may have built an empire, but it was built upon someone else's dreams.

As for my own story, I came into this world at St. Bernadine's Hospital, a place that has witnessed countless beginnings. My entrance was not without its challenges; I faced a myriad of health obstacles that I'll delve into later in this book. My family, second-generation Californians, settled in San Bernardino after my grandparents made the move from Kansas. My grandfather worked for the Santa Fe Railroad, helping to build and maintain the signals that guided trains across the West. I was lucky to spend a lot of time with him, soaking in his stories about the "old days."

His stories were woven with pride and nostalgia, and I learned so much from him—like how to work with my hands or how to create rather than consume. In the 1940s through the 1980s, he climbed the ranks to become a supervisor, ultimately managing a department at the historic Santa Fe station in downtown San Bernardino.

"I'll never forget the excitement when we switched from black and white to color," he would say, laughing. "You kids have it easy!"

My parents also grew up in San Bernardino. My mom was born in the same city that cradled my childhood. My dad, moved to San Bernadino at a young age to live with his mother and became the first entrepreneur in our family—a story I'm eager to share later.

San Bernardino had transformed considerably from the time my grandparents settled there in the 1940s. It was a burgeoning town, home to the massive Norton Air Force Base, which thrived from 1942 until its closure in 1994. It served as the headquarters for the Air Defense Command in Southern California, attracting families and businesses alike. But when the base closed, the city entered a dark chapter, grappling with decline and rising crime.

"Things were different back in the day," my dad would

often lament as we drove through neighborhoods that had seen better times. "It's like the heart of the city was ripped out."

I grew up in the 1970s and 1980s, and by the 1990s, my once vibrant neighborhood had evolved into a more dangerous environment, with gangs migrating from Los Angeles. And so San Bernardino, once a beacon of hope, became synonymous with crime and despair, frequently appearing on lists for the deadliest cities in the United States. The city even filed for bankruptcy, and businesses fled.

Yet my dad's business endured through those tumultuous times, a testament to resilience that I will share later. Despite the challenges, I have countless cherished memories of my hometown. Nestled in a valley and bordered by majestic mountains, the scenery deeply influenced my character. I didn't shy away from the hardships of my health or the struggles of my environment; instead, I transformed them into motivation for change.

Let me share with you the stories that shaped my journey—how I turned my disabilities and God-given talents into stepping stones for success. I hope to inspire you as I recount how it all began.

PART ONE

RUN, ERIC, RUN

RUN, FORREST, RUN

I was on a trip to Savannah, Georgia, for my son's best friend Olivia's wedding, and on the flight I got out my laptop and connected to the Wi-Fi to find a movie to watch. Scrolling through the options, I saw the movie Forrest Gump. As I was watching the movie, my wife, Roxanne, tapped me on the shoulder and handed me her phone. It said, "Savannah, Georgia, Top 10 Tourist Attractions," and one was the park where they filmed *Forrest Gump*. She said, "We should go visit the park while we are there." She looked it up and said it was about five minutes from where we'd be staying. We decided to go see it before all the wedding festivities started. We had a full schedule.

When we arrived in Savannah, it was 100 degrees outside with 90 percent humidity—the kind of day when you need to take multiple showers just to cool down, yet you're still soaked from the humidity. Everyone was dying from the heat and wanted to stay in the air conditioning. We walked to a trolley and made our way downtown to the park where they filmed the story of Forest Gump. I told my family I just wanted to sit on a bench and spend some time reflecting on the Forrest story that I had been talking about for a few years prior. Everyone left to go check out the local shops. I sat on that bench where Tom Hanks filmed the movie and thought about his story and how he narrated it from that bench. Have you seen the movie *Forrest Gump*?

The movie opens with Forrest sharing his life story with a stranger on the park bench. Forrest was at the doctor's office as a little kid with his mom. The doctor was fitting him for leg braces, and the doctor tells Forrest's mom that he needs them because his spine was crooked. As the story progresses and Forrest shares more from the bench, we see Forrest and his best friend, Jenny, walking home from school. The other kids are making fun of Forrest and his leg braces and his disability. Bullies throw dirt at Forrest while they yell at him. They hop on their bikes and chase Forrest and Jenny as they try to get away. At that point, Jenny yells, "Run, Forrest, Run!" If you haven't seen the movie, you have probably heard the phrase "Run, Forrest, Run." Forrest starts running down the driveway to his house as fast as he can with metal leg braces to escape the bullies who were picking on him.

This story is so meaningful to me that I get emotional just telling it. When I was three years old, I wore leg braces just like Forrest. And just like Forrest, my back was crooked too. I did not know at the time that they were going to write a movie about my life! LOL. Just kidding. But all Forrest's adventures are so similar to my life's experiences.

And though I dreamed of running, I could barely walk. Physical and mental disabilities followed me through my childhood.

Today, I feel like Forrest Gump running down that driveway, the braces falling off, and that set the course for the rest of my life—helping others, discovering my purpose and the strength of my leadership, and never giving up. Remember, you don't know when you see someone if they are disabled. Whether it's physical or mental, we all have some sort of disability we are struggling with. If you met me today, you would have no idea I am disabled with a fused spine and metal rods in my back. You wouldn't see the pain I have been through to get where I am today. Please be empathetic to people with disabilities. I share my story to motivate others and to stand up for people everywhere with disabilities. You'll learn how my mindset changed my life.

As I sit down to write this book, I am flooded with memories of the challenges I have faced, particularly the one that shaped me at a young age—my back surgery as a teenager. The physical pain, the mental strain, the uncertainty of it all. . . . It was a difficult time that tested my strength and resilience in ways I never could have imagined.

But through that experience, I gained something invaluable: empathy. It's a quality that I believe sets me apart, that makes me see the world through a different lens. I find myself reacting to situations with kindness and understanding, especially toward those who are vulnerable or in need. I excel in connecting with seniors, disabled individuals, and anyone who requires a little extra care and compassion.

At a business function with my CEO group, we discussed the power of storytelling in branding. I shared how telling my own story has transformed the way people perceive me and my business. It's incredible to see strangers introduce me by recounting my journey, sharing the impact it has had on them. It's humbling and inspiring to know that my story resonates with others, igniting a passion in them to share it with those around them.

Reflecting on my past, I realize that my experience with back surgery has been a guiding force in my life. It has shifted my perspective from a money-driven mindset to one focused on giving back and helping others. The pursuit of success and wealth no longer motivates me as it once did. Instead, the joy of making a difference in someone's life, of lending a hand to those in need, fuels my soul in ways that money never could.

There was a quote I heard once that struck a chord within me: "All other pleasures of life seem to wear out, but the pleasure of helping others in distress never does." It encapsulates the essence of what I have come to understand—that true fulfillment lies in the act of giving, in the ability to uplift and support those around us.

As I embark on this journey of sharing my stories and lessons learned, I hope to inspire others to embrace empathy, kindness, and generosity in their own lives. We all have our struggles and obstacles to overcome, but it's how we respond to them that defines who we are. And through sharing our stories, we can connect, uplift, and inspire one another to be the best versions of ourselves. It all starts with a mindset.

Thank you for joining me here. I hope that my experiences and reflections will resonate with you, and that together, we can create a world filled with empathy, understanding, and kindness. Let us continue to learn from one another, grow together, and spread positivity and compassion wherever we go.

Lessons Learned

- Overcoming personal challenges can develop empathy toward others.
- Your own struggles can develop kindness and compassion for others.

MINDSET

As I sit writing this book of stories, my mind drifts to the intricate tapestry of our minds—the delicate threads that weave together our beliefs, attitudes, and perceptions. It's astonishing how our mindset can dictate not just our thoughts but our very existence. I remember a conversation with one of my mentors. "Eric," he said, leaning back in his chair, "your mindset is like a compass. It doesn't just point you in a direction; it defines the landscape you choose to navigate."

Those words echo in my mind as I reflect on the different types of mindsets that color our experiences. There's the growth mindset, that steadfast belief that we can evolve, learn, and expand our horizons. Then there's the fixed mindset, a stubborn anchor that weighs us down, convincing us that we are who we are and cannot change. I have danced between these mindsets more times than I care to admit, feeling the weight of limitations pressing against my chest.

"Why do you think some people thrive while others merely survive?" I once asked my mentor, the question hanging heavy in the air.

"Ah," he replied, his voice a gentle rumble, "it's all in how they perceive their world. Those with an abundance mindset see opportunities where others see obstacles. They believe in possibilities, while the poverty mindset constricts the spirit, blurring the horizon."

The lessons of mindset seeped into my bones over the years. I learned that a good leader understands the importance of continuous learning and the necessity of an open mind. With every experience, my mindset shaped not only my capacity for growth but also the environment around me. I could feel it. When I entered a room, my energy was contagious, a silent force that could uplift or deflate the spirits of those present.

I recall vivid moments standing before my team, where the energy was palpable. "Alright, team!" I'd say, a smile breaking across my face. "Let's turn this day around!" If I walked in with low energy, dragging my feet and wearing a frown, the atmosphere would thicken like molasses, weighing everyone down. But when I strode in buoyant and smiling, the room would light up. Laughter would ripple through the air, and suddenly, we were all buoyed by a shared sense of purpose.

"You see the difference?" I would often remind them. "Our mindsets are contagious. We have the power to influence not only our own mood but also the energy of everyone around us."

And it's true—every thought we entertain sends ripples throughout our bodies. Science tells us that our thoughts can trigger neurochemical changes, lifting our spirits with a surge of dopamine when we practice gratitude. I've learned that every cell in our body is replaced every two months, a remarkable opportunity to reprogram ourselves towards optimism through mindfulness and gratitude.

So, I ask myself: Which room do I want to walk into? The one filled with shadows of despair or a vibrant space illuminated by hope and enthusiasm? As a leader, I realize the power is in my hands, and I must set my mind for success.

Lessons Learned

- Our beliefs and attitudes define our experiences and interactions. Mindset shapes our reality.
- Energy is contagious. A leader's mindset influences the mood and energy of the entire room.

THE POWER OF FAITH AND MINDSET

Everyone in the world has some sort of disability, whether it's physical, mental, or emotional. Some are more apparent than others, while others are hidden beneath the surface. I, myself, have faced many challenges due to my disabilities, but I have always been a firm believer in the power of the mind to overcome any obstacle.

I have seen firsthand the incredible strength that lies within each and every one of us. A few years ago, my father-in-law, Tom, was on the brink of death. He was recovering from brain surgery, but the doctors had given up hope, and his vitals were showing that there was no chance of survival. He had accepted his fate and was at peace with the idea of passing on.

But then something miraculous happened. My wife, Roxanne, the person he was closest to, sat by his bedside and pleaded with him to keep fighting. She told him that he was needed, that his presence in this world was important, and that she couldn't bear to lose him. It was a heartfelt plea, filled with love and desperation.

And you know what? It worked. The next day, against all odds, Tom was removed from life support and began to show signs of improvement. The doctors were baffled, unable to explain how or why this sudden turnaround had occurred.

But I knew in my heart that it was the power of the mind and faith.

Tom had made a conscious decision to live, to fight against the odds and defy the expectations of those around them. And his body responded in kind, healing itself in a way that no medical intervention could ever explain.

This experience taught me a valuable lesson: We are capable of so much more than we realize if our mindset is good. Our thoughts and beliefs have the power to shape our reality, to overcome even the most insurmountable obstacles. It was a reminder that we are not powerless in the face of adversity, but rather, we hold the key to our own healing and success.

I want my personal story to serve as a beacon of hope for anyone facing their own challenges. I want them to know that they are not alone, that they have the strength and resilience within them to overcome whatever obstacles stand in their way. And most importantly, I want them to remember that they are capable of creating their own miracles, simply by believing in the power of their own mind.

I have witnessed firsthand the incredible transformation that can occur when we tap into the power of our minds. Tom's story is proof—our mindset is a force that can defy logic and surpass all expectations. The human spirit is a resilient and powerful thing, capable of achieving the impossible when fueled by determination and belief.

As I reflect on that moment in the hospital room, watching as my loved one defied death itself, I am reminded of the profound impact our thoughts and intentions can have on our physical being. It's a reminder that we are not bound by the limitations that others may place upon us, but rather have the ability to rewrite our own narratives and transcend any obstacle that stands in our way.

The power of the mind is a force to be reckoned with, a source of strength and healing that lies dormant within each and every one of us. It is a reminder that we are the masters of our own destinies, capable of shaping our lives in ways that defy all expectations. And it is my hope that by sharing my story, others will be inspired to tap into their own inner strength and harness the power of their own minds to create miracles of their own.

Lessons Learned

- Personal connections and heartfelt support from loved ones can inspire strength and motivation in times of struggle. Emotional bonds can play a crucial role in overcoming obstacles.
- We have the ability to rewrite our own narratives and transcend limitations. By believing in ourselves and the power of our minds, we can create our own miracles and achieve the seemingly impossible.

AFFLICTIONS FOR LIFE

Growing up, I faced a myriad of challenges that tested my strength and resilience. From a young age, I struggled with dyslexia, which made reading, writing, and math difficult for me. I was placed in special education classes in elementary school, where I often felt isolated and different from my peers. Additionally, issues with my back required me to wear leg braces starting at a young age. These physical limitations made simple tasks like walking and running a struggle for me.

As if that wasn't enough, I was also dealing with a debilitating condition that worsened over time. Despite the physical pain and emotional toll, I refused to give up.

The combination of these afflictions took a toll on my self-esteem, leading to feelings of anxiety and depression. I constantly felt like I was fighting an uphill battle, never quite measuring up to the expectations of others. However, everything changed after my back surgery. I was given a second chance at life, and I was determined to make the most of it.

I adopted a new outlook on life, one filled with positivity and determination. I refused to let my disabilities define me or hold me back. Instead, I used them as motivation to push myself harder and strive for success. I embraced the belief that anything is possible if you set your mind to it, and I made it my mission to prove the naysayers wrong. I love the quote: "Success is the best revenge."

I refuse to let anyone tell me what I could or couldn't do. I dedicated myself to mastering new skills and overcoming obstacles, no matter how daunting they seemed. Through hard work and perseverance, I was able to achieve things that others thought were impossible for someone like me.

As I grew older, my definition of success evolved. It wasn't about money or power anymore. True success, I realized, was about making a difference in the lives of others and fostering genuine, meaningful relationships. I found fulfillment in helping people and inspiring them to reach their full potential.

I learned that success truly is the best revenge. By proving my doubters wrong and showing the world what I was capable of, I was able to inspire others to do the same. My journey from a struggling, insecure child to a confident, resilient adult taught me that with determination and perseverance, anything is possible. And I made it my mission to share that message with the world, to show others that they too can overcome their own challenges and achieve greatness.

Lessons Learned

- Never let others' negative perceptions define your worth or capabilities.
- Success is not measured by material possessions, but by the impact you have on others.

ENTREPRENEURSHIP, MY JOURNEY

From a young age, entrepreneurship was a fundamental part of my life, thanks to my parents, both of whom owned their own businesses. My father, Terry, ran his own company, Chem-Pak, while my mother, Debbie, was a partner in hers. This environment shaped my understanding of work and ambition, as I often found myself in their offices, absorbing the hustle and bustle of their entrepreneurial endeavors. Eventually I worked for my father's company, taking on various roles from delivery driver to outside sales. It was an invaluable learning experience that deepened my understanding of business operations and sales.

After my surgery in high school, I decided to channel my love for cars into a car detailing business. With my father being an avid car enthusiast and a network of friends who owned luxury vehicles, I found my niche. Armed with flyers and business cards, I began offering my services to local neighbors, detailing everything from Mercedes to Ferraris. Though it was a small start, it ignited my passion for entrepreneurship and set the stage for future endeavors.

In college, I partnered with my best friend, Dave, to start a carpet cleaning business. My father, who had connections in the janitorial supply industry, helped us secure a contract with 3M company for their popular Scotchgard service. We became certified and began receiving calls from their corporation, sending us out to ensure customers' upholstery was properly treated. By the time I was in my early twenties, we had built the business to a point where we could sell it, marking another milestone in my entrepreneurial journey.

Shortly thereafter, a family friend who owned a large contract cleaning company approached me. He needed someone to manage his inland division, and my father had recommended me. I took on the challenge, learning the ins and outs of running a business and managing teams. Eventually, when the division grew, I bought it with a few partners, expanding on the foundation we had built.

There was a time when I was juggling multiple jobs to prepare for my wedding. I was working at the contract cleaning company during the night and doing sales for my father's business during the day. To make ends meet, I even took a job at Coco's restaurant on the weekends. I remember vividly the moment I reached my financial goal for the wedding; I walked into the restaurant and told the general manager, "I quit." Surprised, he asked why. I simply replied, "I've made the amount of money I need to make, and I don't need this job anymore."

So much of this goes back to my father, Terry, a truly natural entrepreneur and salesman. He obviously played a crucial role in kickstarting my own entrepreneurial journey at an early age, a story I'll share later. His mindset—focused on transforming his life and building a business—is something he instilled in me. I vividly recall him saying that while he could teach anyone the mechanics of selling, he couldn't make someone a salesman. He believed that true salesmanship begins with passion and heart. To be authentic, you must genuinely believe in the product or service you're selling; if you don't have faith in it, you can't expect others to. Moreover, you can't risk everything to build a business unless you believe in yourself and your capabilities.

My grandmother once said my father could sell ice to Eskimos because of his fervor for his work. From an early age, he recognized that he didn't want to work for someone else; he wanted to steer his own destiny. He often recounted how, in his early twenties while working at a furniture store, he encountered numerous sales representatives who were building relationships and earning well for their efforts. This experience inspired him to pursue a career in sales. After being hired by a manufacturer in the cleaning industry, he met many independent distributors of cleaning supplies who drove luxury cars and wore tailored suits. This observation ignited his ambition to learn more about starting his own janitorial distribution company.

In 1987, he founded Chem-Pak with a mission to provide essential products for businesses: janitorial supplies, office goods, paper products, and chemicals. My grandparents supported him as investors, loaning him the funds to launch the company. He benefited from the mentorship of industry veterans and other business owners who offered invaluable advice. My mother often shared how challenging it was for our family to live on her income while my father built his business. Even as a child, I witnessed his relentless work ethic; I remember him selling during the day, returning home in the late afternoon to order products, pack orders in his van, and deliver everything himself. In the beginning, it was a one-man show. Despite his nonstop work, I never felt neglected, as he always welcomed my help when I wanted to pitch in. Once he expanded the business and secured a warehouse,

I started by sweeping floors and cleaning. When I was old enough, I helped set up his first computer system and later became a delivery driver before moving into sales.

Over the years, my father imparted many lessons that have stayed with me. Two major ones stand out: First, build a reputation in your industry and become an expert in your field. This fosters credibility and positions you as a respected industry leader. When I began doing insurance sales for a neighbor while also working in my father's company, I was advised to choose one path and master it. The message was clear: You don't want to be the person selling insurance on the side to make extra cash. Focus on succeeding in your current role, and you won't need a side hustle. He was right! The second lesson was to avoid worrying about what others are doing. Instead, do your best and invest in your own growth. Learn from others, build your skills, but resist the urge to compete with anyone else.

In a recent podcast interview, I shared our family business story and spoke about my father. I recounted a moment when a competitor opened a location directly across the street from us. I was shocked and asked my father what we would do. He calmly replied that we wouldn't concern ourselves with their actions; we would continue building relationships in the community, just as we always had. The competitor became fixated on our every move—lowering their prices, visiting our location, and engaging with our customers. Yet my father remained unfazed, sticking to his strategy. Eventually, the other company went out of business, and here we are, thirty-eight years later, still thriving. My father always led by example, which is something I deeply admire.

He taught me hard lessons that I didn't fully appreciate

until I grew older and wiser. Looking back, I now understand his motivations and how they shaped who I am today. One final story illustrates how he passed his work ethic down to me. Nothing was ever handed to me; I had to earn it. My children often say I'm harder on family than on others because I genuinely want to see them succeed. At one point, I was working in sales and had just bought my first home and a new car. My income fluctuated due to commission, and I didn't plan well, leading to my first low sales month. When I received my paycheck, I immediately realized I hadn't earned enough to cover my expenses. I approached my father for help. While he was understanding, he told me I needed to work harder and that he wouldn't lend me any money.

Panicked, I explained my situation to my mother, who eventually agreed to help me with a loan, but that was just between us. I was anxious about what would happen if I had another low month. Determined, I worked harder than ever and secured a significant account. The following month, I made more money than I ever had and landed one of the company's largest customers. When he handed me the sizable check, my father said, "Do you see now why I didn't help you with a loan? I knew you wouldn't let yourself get into that position again; you would work to support yourself." And I did. It was a tough lesson but one that has served me well ever since.

Lessons Learned

- Growing up in an entrepreneurial family can instill a lifelong passion for business. Embrace your roots!
- Identifying and pursuing your interests can lead to successful ventures, even at a young age.

NAVIGATING LIFE'S CHALLENGES

Like everyone, I have had obstacles in my life. In the roller-coaster ride of life, there are bound to be ups and downs, twists and turns, that can throw us off balance. But I have always believed in facing challenges head-on, navigating through obstacles with a calm and collected demeanor that has served me well in both my personal life and in the business world.

I have chosen never to let things get under my skin, to let the weight of the world crush me. Instead, I have always looked at the bigger picture, knowing that every hurdle is a learning opportunity, a chance to become stronger and wiser. I don't stress about the things I cannot control; I don't waste my energy on anger or frustration. I simply give it all up to a higher power and trust that everything will fall into place.

This mindset has not only helped me weather the storms of life but has also translated seamlessly into my approach to leadership in the business world. As a leader, I have always believed in leading by example, in showing my team that obstacles are just temporary roadblocks that can be overcome with determination and a positive attitude.

When faced with challenges in business, I have always preached a simple yet powerful mantra to my team: "I don't want excuses; I want solutions." I don't want to hear about how or why we got into a sticky situation; I want to know how we are going to fix it and move forward. Dwelling on the past or playing the blame game will only hinder our progress.

By embracing a mindset of acceptance, positivity, and problem-solving, I have been able to steer my businesses through rough waters and come out on the other side stronger and more resilient. And I know that no matter what life throws my way, I will always find a way to navigate through it with grace and determination.

Lessons Learned

- Trust in a higher power to guide you through difficult times.
- Lead by example and demonstrate resilience in the face of adversity.
- Encourage your team to adopt a proactive problem-solving approach rather than making excuses or assigning blame.

FROM PHYSICAL TO MENTAL DISABILITIES: DYSLEXIA

In first grade, I faced a pivotal moment that would shape my educational journey in ways I could never have anticipated. I was held back a year, a decision that left me feeling isolated as my friends moved ahead into the next grade without me. This setback not only disrupted my academic progression but also severed the bonds I had with my peers. Back then, being held back meant something entirely different than it does now; it carried a stigma that lingered long after the decision was made.

The reason for my retention was multilayered. I had already been grappling with physical challenges, navigating life with leg braces and dealing with the complications of a back condition that marked me disabled. Yet, what often went unnoticed were the struggles I faced mentally. I found myself in special education classes, struggling with the basic building blocks of learning—reading and math. Letters danced on the page, and words often appeared backward to me. I could turn a book upside down and read it fluently, but I wrestled with traditional reading and writing. Phonetic spelling became my crutch; I could communicate, but the words I wrote rarely resembled their proper forms.

Math was an even greater hurdle. Numbers eluded me, and I felt a profound sense of frustration as I failed to grasp concepts that seemed so straightforward to my classmates. Ultimately, testing confirmed that I had severe dyslexia. Learning this diagnosis was a double-edged sword; it explained my struggles but also added to the weight of feeling different and inadequate amid my peers. I carried the burden of not just one disability but two, and I felt the sting of being left behind both academically and socially.

My mother emerged as my strongest advocate during this challenging time. She arranged for private tutoring and sought specialized classes in reading and math, determined to help me overcome these obstacles. Her unwavering support was invaluable, yet the emotional toll was significant. I often felt singled out, a target for teasing because I didn't participate in regular recess or classes. The label of being in "special ed" set me apart from my peers and deepened my feelings of isolation.

As I moved through elementary school and into junior high, I continued to grapple with my learning challenges. Eventually, I underwent surgery that altered my physical issues, but it was my late teens and early twenties that marked a turning point in my understanding of dyslexia. During this time I began to explore the narratives of famous individuals who, like me, faced severe dyslexia yet achieved remarkable success. Names like Albert Einstein, Thomas Edison, and even contemporary figures like Elon Musk began to populate my mind. I discovered that these luminaries had transformed their perceived limitations into incredible strengths.

This realization was empowering. I began to embrace my dyslexia as a unique aspect of my identity, a "superpower" that allowed me to think differently. I found new ways to approach math; while traditional methods eluded me, I developed my own strategies for calculation. I learned to add and multiply numbers in my head, using techniques that felt intuitive to me, even if they didn't align with conventional practices.

By my mid-twenties, I had retrained my brain to see the world through a different lens. The emotional weight of my early struggles began to lift, replaced by a sense of pride in my ability to learn in ways that worked for me. I realized that my journey, though fraught with challenges, had equipped me with a perspective that few others shared.

Today, I view my dyslexia not as a hindrance but as a vital part of my story—a testament to resilience, adaptation, and growth. My experience has taught me that our differences can be our greatest strengths, and that embracing them can lead to unexpected paths of success. As I reflect on this journey, I am reminded that the struggles I faced in those early years have ultimately shaped me into the person I am today, someone who sees the world differently and approaches learning with an open heart and mind. I often say now, "My disabilities don't define me; they motivate me!"

Lessons Learned

- Having supportive advocates, like my parents, can make a significant difference in overcoming obstacles. Their dedication to finding the right resources and support systems was essential to my growth and success.
- Success is not a one-size-fits-all concept. By developing my own methods for learning and problem-solving, I discovered that there is more than one way to reach a goal, and what works for one person may not work for another.

GOOD COMPANY

If you have dyslexia like me, you're in good company! Many brilliant minds and creative spirits throughout history have navigated similar challenges and gone on to leave their mark on the world. Dyslexia, although often misunderstood, can foster unique perspectives and innovative thinking. Here's a lighthearted look at fifteen famous individuals who have not only embraced their dyslexia but also transformed it into a driving force for their success.

1. Albert Einstein

Often labeled as a late talker, Einstein faced significant struggles with communication and social interactions during his early years. While he adored math and science, he found grammar and spelling to be quite the uphill battle. Although he was never formally diagnosed with dyslexia, his ability to see the world through a distinctive lens—potentially shaped by his dyslexia—led to groundbreaking scientific breakthroughs.

2. Henry Ford

The visionary behind the Ford Motor Company and the creator of the iconic Model T, Ford revolutionized manufacturing with his assembly line approach. Despite facing difficulties with reading and schoolwork, he excelled in engineering, proving that practical skills can often outweigh traditional academic challenges.

3. Richard Branson

Branson has been an outspoken advocate for those with dyslexia, sharing how it shaped his education and fueled his entrepreneurial spirit. He attributes his success to a knack for creative thinking and a willingness to delegate tasks he finds challenging. Leaving school at just fifteen didn't stop him from building a thriving business empire—talk about defying the odds!

4. Steven Spielberg

Diagnosed with dyslexia as an adult, Spielberg faced bullying during his school years but found solace in filmmaking. He transformed his challenges into a source of creativity, viewing dyslexia as a unique hurdle that enhances his imagination and resilience—qualities that shine through in his legendary films.

5. Whoopi Goldberg

Goldberg's journey with undiagnosed dyslexia made her school years particularly challenging. However, as an adult, she learned to embrace different learning styles, which contributed to her diverse and successful career in entertainment. Her story is a testament to adaptability and self-acceptance.

6. Leonardo da Vinci

Though historical records don't confirm a diagnosis, many believe that da Vinci may have had dyslexia, as evidenced by his mirror writing and spelling inconsistencies. His inventive genius and exceptional visual-spatial skills are often linked with dyslexia, showcasing that creativity can flourish even in the face of learning challenges.

7. Cher

The legendary Cher faced significant hurdles in school before her dyslexia was identified. She has candidly discussed her struggles with reading scripts, ultimately developing clever memorization techniques that helped her thrive in her illustrious career.

8. Orlando Bloom

Diagnosed with dyslexia at an early age, Bloom openly shares the challenges he faced in his education. However, he credits his dyslexia with helping him hone a robust work ethic and creative problem-solving skills, both vital to his success as an actor.

9. Tom Cruise

Early education was a challenge for Cruise due to his dyslexia, which made reading and writing particularly tough. He has bravely shared his journey of overcoming these obstacles, illustrating how determination and adaptability can lead to remarkable achievements in the acting world.

10. Keira Knightley

Diagnosed with dyslexia as a child, Knightley faced her share of school-related struggles. However, her passion for acting served as motivation to improve her reading and writing skills, using scripts as a fun and effective practice tool.

11. Dav Pilkey

The beloved author and illustrator of children's literature, Dav Pilkey proudly claims that dyslexia is his superpower. His experiences not only shaped him as a writer but also made him an inspiring role model for children around the globe, proving that challenges can lead to creativity.

12. Patricia Polacco

Renowned for her contributions to children's literature, Polacco didn't learn to read until she was fourteen. She lived with undiagnosed dyslexia until a compassionate teacher recognized her unique learning style and helped her discover the joy of reading.

13. Anderson Cooper

The esteemed journalist and CNN anchor struggled with dyslexia in his youth but didn't let it hinder his ambitions. He has spoken about how his distinctive perspective and ability to think differently have been instrumental in his success in the fast-paced world of journalism.

14. Pablo Picasso

While Picasso was never officially diagnosed, many experts believe he exhibited traits of dyslexia. His unconventional artistic perspectives and tendency to think outside the box are hallmarks of a creative mind that possibly navigated the world through a different lens.

15. Robin Williams

The late beloved actor and comedian faced dyslexia throughout his life. He ingeniously used comedy as a coping mechanism for his reading and writing challenges, ultimately becoming one of the most successful entertainers of all time. His legacy reminds us that laughter can be a powerful tool for overcoming adversity.

These remarkable individuals have shown that dyslexia is not a barrier but rather a unique perspective that can lead to extraordinary achievements. So, here's to embracing our quirks and celebrating the incredible contributions that come from thinking differently!

FAMILY TIES

From the moment I stepped foot in elementary school, it was clear that I was different from the other kids. While they lugged around colorful backpacks filled with their books and snacks, I stood out as the only one carrying a well-worn, professional briefcase. It was a sight to behold—a young boy with a briefcase in tow, ready to take on the world.

But that's just who I was. Ever since I can remember, I had been drawn to the idea of hard work and success. And a lot of it stemmed from one source of inspiration—Michael J. Fox's character, Alex P. Keaton, on the popular show *Family Ties*. His disciplined, businesslike demeanor resonated with me in a way that nothing else did. He embodied everything I aspired to be: independent, hardworking, and unafraid to stand out.

People started calling me "Alex" after his character, and I wore that nickname like a badge of honor. It was a reminder of my determination to carve my own path, even if it meant straying from the norm. While some may have raised eyebrows at my choice to carry a briefcase, I never faltered in my belief that it was okay to be different.

As I journeyed through elementary school and into middle school, my briefcase became more than just a practical accessory; it became a symbol of my faith in myself. I learned early on that standing out from the crowd was not something to be feared, but rather embraced. It took courage to be true to myself—to follow my own path even when it diverged from the norm. And with each passing day, I grew more confident in my decision.

So here's to you, Alex P. Keaton. Thank you for showing me the power of believing in myself, for teaching me that it's okay to be different, and for inspiring a young boy to never be afraid to stand out. My briefcase may have been unconventional, but it was a reflection of my unwavering belief that anything is possible when you have the courage to be yourself.

Lessons Learned

- Have the courage to think for yourself and follow your own path with confidence.
- Believe in your abilities and have faith in your own potential for success.
- Remember that it's okay to be different and that true strength lies in embracing your individuality.

THE HEART OF THE MATTER

In the summer of 2010, while sitting on my driveway, the sun beating down on me, I felt an unsettling chill run through my body. My heart raced uncontrollably, pounding against my chest like a wild beast desperate to escape. I felt lightheaded and dizzy, and a wave of panic washed over me. "I don't feel good," I told my wife, who had just stepped out to check on me. "I think I need to go to the hospital."

The ambulance arrived in a flurry of lights and sirens, and as they loaded me on the stretcher, I felt a mix of fear and relief. Fear of what was happening to me, and relief that I might finally get some answers.

At the hospital, the sterile smell of antiseptic hung thick in the air. A nurse rushed to take my blood pressure, her brow furrowing as the numbers flashed on the screen. "This is really high," she muttered, exchanging glances with the doctor.

"Have you experienced any pain?" he asked, his voice steady but concerned.

"No," I replied, barely able to catch my breath. "Just this racing heart."

As they ran a series of tests, I felt a sense of dread settle in my stomach. They gave me a shot to bring my blood pressure down, but it plummeted too low, and the world around me faded to black.

When I came to, I was connected to machines beeping and

humming around me. "You didn't have a heart attack," the doctor said. Relief flooded through me, but then he added, "Your heart rate is extremely elevated. We need to get it under control."

They referred me to my primary care doctor, and the cycle of appointments began. At each visit, I faced the same grim reality: My blood pressure and heart rate were alarmingly high. "You have white coat syndrome," my doctor reassured me. "It's common; many people get anxious in a doctor's office." But I knew it was more than that. I was prescribed beta-blockers and blood pressure medication, but the side effects were debilitating. Every time I took them, I felt like I was fading away; I was lethargic and detached from reality.

"I don't know how much longer I can live like this," I told my wife one evening, my voice heavy with despair. "I feel trapped in my own body."

After months of suffering, a friend who was a vice president at UCLA Medical Center suggested I see a specialist. My wife and I made the trip to Los Angeles, feeling hopeful yet anxious; it was like my childhood all over again. As I sat in the specialist's office, I explained my struggles. The doctor listened intently, nodding in understanding. "I think you have extreme tachycardia," he said, his voice calm yet firm. "It's a condition called P.V.C. Your heart rate is too high at rest, and every activity sends it into overdrive."

I felt a mix of relief and dread. I wasn't alone in this struggle; my doctor understood. He had experienced similar issues and knew how it felt. But the path forward seemed daunting. "We need to increase your beta-blockers," he said, and I braced myself for the side effects that would follow.

For five long years, I battled this condition. I felt like a prisoner in my own body, constantly anxious about the next episode. I was in and out of emergency rooms, each time thinking, *Is this the moment I'll have a heart attack?* But each time, the tests would come back clear—no heart attack, just high numbers.

One day, during a particularly low moment, a friend of mine—a PE teacher and avid cyclist, asked me, "Have you ever cycled?" he asked, a spark of excitement in his voice. "Change your diet, do some research on what helps the heart, and see if cycling helps."

Skeptical but desperate, I took his advice. I cut out caffeine, eliminated chocolate, prioritized sleep, minimized stress, and committed to daily exercise. I started cycling with him, and it transformed my life in ways I never expected.

As I pedaled through the fresh air, I felt a sense of freedom I hadn't experienced in years. The rhythm of my heart began to change; it was still there, but I learned to appreciate the moments of stillness between the racing. I discovered that if I focused on my breathing and practiced mindfulness, I could control my heart rate.

I realized that I could feel the racing start, and instead of panicking, I'd sit, breathe, and remind myself that I had the power to bring it down. I was no longer a victim of my condition; I was its master.

Through this journey, I learned that mental resilience was just as crucial as physical health. I discovered that my mind held the key to controlling my body. It was a profound realization: If I approached my heart condition with calm and control, I could live my life without the constant fear of what might happen next.

Now, I live with my condition, but it doesn't define me.

I've learned to accept it as part of my life, a challenge that I manage every day. I don't panic when my heart races; I acknowledge it and remind myself that I've been here before.

In the years since that tumultuous summer of 2010, my journey has been one of profound transformation. I have learned to live with my heart condition, not as a burden but as a part of my story. Each day presents its own challenges, but I face them with a newfound resilience, a steady resolve that comes from understanding my own body and mind.

As I continue to cycle and stay active, I find joy in the simple act of movement. The wind against my face, the rhythm of my pedals, and the sense of freedom on the open road remind me that I am alive and capable. I've also learned to listen to my body, to recognize when it needs rest, and to give myself grace when things feel overwhelming.

Moreover, I've become an advocate for mental health awareness, understanding how intertwined our mental and physical well-being truly are. I share my story with others who might be struggling with their health, encouraging them to seek help and not shy away from the difficult conversations. I remind them that they are not alone in their battles.

Today, I approach life with a sense of gratitude. I appreciate the moments of stillness as much as the bursts of excitement. I've discovered that life is not just about overcoming obstacles but also about embracing the journey—every twist and turn, every setback and triumph.

Through all of this, I've come to understand that our greatest battles often lie within us. The heart may race, and anxiety may rise, but we have the power to reclaim our lives. I choose to live boldly, with purpose and intention, knowing that I can control my mind and, in turn, my body.

Lessons Learned

- Seek support; don't hesitate to reach out for help. Whether it's from friends, family, or professionals, support can lead to new perspectives and solutions.
- Embrace changes in your lifestyle that can improve your health. Small adjustments in diet and exercise can make a huge difference.

ANXIETY: FROM MY HEART TO MY MIND

Today, my heart condition is under control, and I have not experienced an episode in years. But more than that, I have found a new purpose in using my experience to help others. As a corporate leader, I understand the profound impact that mental health and wellness can have on a team. I have seen firsthand how my mood and demeanor can set the tone for the entire company, influencing the attitudes and behaviors of those around me.

Through workshops and guidance, I strive to impart the lessons I have learned, emphasizing the importance of maintaining a positive mindset and outlook, even in the face of adversity. I have come to realize that as a leader, my actions speak louder than words, and by embodying a sense of calm and positivity, I can inspire and uplift those around me.

It has been a challenging journey, fraught with obstacles and setbacks, but through it all, I have emerged stronger and more resilient. I have learned that true leadership is not just about making tough decisions or driving results, but about creating a culture of empathy, understanding, and support. And in doing so, I have found a sense of fulfillment and purpose that goes beyond any professional accolades or achievements.

Lessons Learned

- Learning to manage stress and anxiety through meditation, breathing exercises, and mental focus can have a profound effect on overall well-being.
- Medication and lifestyle changes can be effective tools in managing chronic health conditions.
- As a leader, one's mood and demeanor can set the tone for the entire team and influence the overall atmosphere of the workplace.

CLAUSTROPHOBIA FOR A MIND SHIFT

It was a family trip to Hawaii that forever altered my relationship with flying. I remember the sweltering heat of the tarmac and the unsettling stillness inside the plane as we sat grounded for what felt like an eternity. Four long hours ticked by, each minute stretching my nerves taut. A woman, fraught with her own mental anguish, was seated just in front of us. Her anxious energy was palpable, infectious even, as she spiraled deeper into panic over a crisis back home with her son. She was yelling and screaming the whole time.

As the heat enveloped us, I could sense my own claustrophobia creeping in, tightening its grip around my chest. I had mentally prepared for a four-hour flight, but the unexpected delay turned this journey into an eight-hour ordeal. I was trapped, and my mind raced with thoughts of panic. The realization that there was no escape only intensified my discomfort. I couldn't shake the feeling that I was suffocating, trapped in that metal tube with no way out.

When we finally landed at LAX, I was a bundle of frayed nerves. The woman was still in a daze, oblivious to the chaos of the flight she had just endured. As she stumbled off the plane, I turned to my wife, declaring, "I'm done. I'm never flying again." In that moment, I meant every word. I had reached my limit, and I didn't step foot on a plane for nine long years.

During that time, I drove my family across the country, enduring grueling hours on the road instead of facing my fears in the air. The control I felt while driving was a comfort; I could stop whenever I pleased, open the door, and escape if I needed to. But planes were a different beast altogether—elevators too. The thought of being confined in a space with no escape was enough to send me spiraling into anxiety.

However, life has a funny way of pushing you toward growth. When my son moved to New York, I was once again faced with the choice: drive for days or conquer my fears and fly. My wife, my steadfast supporter, gently reminded me of the impact my fears had on her life. "It's not fair to me," she said, her voice filled with both understanding and frustration. I realized then that my decision to avoid flying was limiting her experiences as well. I couldn't bear the thought of holding her back any longer.

That conversation was a turning point. I knew I had to confront my fears, not just for myself but for my family. I began taking short flights—each one a small step toward reclaiming my freedom. Friends suggested medications or even alcohol to ease the anxiety, but I needed a different approach. I turned to prayer, seeking solace and strength from my faith. I used my mindset to curb my fear.

On my first flight back, I clasped my wife's hand and prayed. I asked for peace, for the anxiety to melt away, and for courage to face the journey ahead. Miraculously, I felt a shift. Each subsequent flight became easier. I found myself flying cross-country, visiting places I had longed to see—Rhode Island, Chicago, New Orleans, and more. Each trip reaffirmed my faith and my commitment to overcoming my fears.

By the end of the year, my wife jokingly complained that I had become the frequent flyer in our family. "You're running me ragged!" she laughed, marveling at how far I had come. And yet, it wasn't just the travel that had changed; it was me. The last flight we took back from New York was a reminder of how far I had journeyed. My wife, feeling the familiar twinge of anxiety, turned to me, and in that moment, I found myself holding her hand, praying once more, reminding her that it was all mental.

Now, as I look forward to trips planned for Fiji, Australia, and Tuscany, I realize that my faith and mindset has been the cornerstone of my transformation. I learned that the battle against claustrophobia was not just about overcoming fear; it was about trusting in something greater than myself. It's another example of how your mindset can change your life. Once I had my mind under control, I could experience so many amazing places and things. This has happened many times in my life.

Lessons Learned

- Open communication with loved ones can help reveal how personal struggles impact those around us, allowing for collective growth.
- Taking small, manageable steps toward facing fears can lead to significant breakthroughs over time.

MY SWISS AWAKENING–CHANGING OUR OUTLOOK

As I reflect, I can't help but think about how much we are products of our circumstances. Growing up, I was shaped by my upbringing, my beliefs, and the environment around me. Like many, I held biases and prejudices that I'd learned without question. There was a time when I was closed off to ideas and people who didn't fit the mold of what I thought was "normal."

But everything began to change because of my son, Grant, who opened my eyes to a world beyond my own limited understanding.

I was raised in a Southern Baptist household, where certain ideologies were ingrained in me from an early age. I remember the conversations, often laced with judgment and misconceptions, about those who lived differently or loved differently. I carried these beliefs into adulthood, feeling justified in my opinions.

But then Grant came into my life. As he grew up, he began to challenge everything I thought I understood about love, acceptance, and what it means to be truly open-minded. I remember one moment vividly. Grant was in his teenage years, and he sat me down one evening and said, his voice steady but filled with conviction, "Dad, you need to understand that love is love, no matter who it's between."

Those words struck me deeply, igniting a spark of curiosity in me that I had buried for far too long.

In 2006 my wife, my parents, and I embarked on a journey to Switzerland for a business trip that turned into a life-changing experience. It was my first time traveling outside the country, and I was both excited and apprehensive. I didn't realize then how transformative this trip would be.

We arrived in Switzerland, and the moment I set foot on the shores of Lake Geneva, I felt a sense of peace wash over me. The majestic mountains stood like guardians around the lake, and the air was crisp and clean. I remember thinking, "Is this what it feels like to escape the noise of everyday life?"

During our trip, we had the opportunity to meet various people in the industry while attending a conference. I was eager to connect and learn, but what I found most intriguing was how different the Swiss mindset was compared to what I was used to back in California.

One evening, as we shared a meal with some locals, I was struck by how they talked about their lives. When I mentioned the political climate back home, they looked at me with a mix of confusion and indifference. "We don't really follow American politics," one man said, shrugging his shoulders. "It's just not our concern." It was as if they were living in a bubble, free from the chaos and divisions that seemed to consume so much of the world.

As the days passed, we traveled through the Swiss Alps, explored the enchanting streets of Montreux on the shores of Lake Geneva. Each experience deepened my appreciation for their culture—their tranquility, their neutrality, and their profound sense of community. I realized that their happiness wasn't derived from material wealth or political power, but rather from a collective understanding of living in harmony with one another, free from the burdens of judgment.

I returned home with a renewed perspective, one that prompted me to think critically about the beliefs I had held for so long. I began to understand that many people are simply a product of their upbringing, shaped by the narratives they've been taught. This realization led me to an important epiphany: If I wanted to embrace a more inclusive world, I would first have to confront my own biases and allow myself to learn from others.

This journey of understanding was put to the test when I encountered a book assigned for my master's program about manhood. The author's views were antiquated and rigid, discussing how men should be warriors and cowboys, shunning any traits deemed feminine. As I attempted to read through the first chapter, I felt an overwhelming sense of frustration.

"This is not what I believe," I muttered to myself, shaking my head. The author's rigid definitions clashed with everything I had learned from Grant, who had shown me that masculinity could be tender, that strength didn't have to be synonymous with aggression.

I remember sharing my struggle with my family. "It's the first time I've ever read something and felt so disconnected from the author's arguments," I confessed. "I couldn't finish it because I just don't agree with his view of what a man should be."

My family listened, and I could see the understanding in their eyes. They knew the journey I'd been on, the walls I'd torn down within myself. "You're evolving, Dad," Grant said gently. "That's okay. It means you're growing."

As I reflected on my journey, I realized that being

open-minded is not merely about accepting different beliefs; it's about actively engaging with them, understanding their origins, and allowing them to challenge your own. It requires vulnerability, the willingness to admit that you may have been wrong, and the courage to embrace new perspectives.

In the years since my trip to Switzerland, I've committed myself to this journey of open-mindedness. I've sought out diverse experiences, engaged with people from all walks of life, and continually challenged my own beliefs. I've learned to listen more than speak, to ask questions rather than make assumptions, and to foster connections based on respect and understanding.

As I look back on my life, I recognize that the journey of self-discovery is never truly finished. It's a continuous process of learning, unlearning, and growing. And while I may not have all the answers, I am proud to say that I approach the world with an open heart and a curious mind.

Lessons Learned

- Approach conversations with an open mind, listen to others' experiences, and be willing to learn from them.
- Recognize that everyone is a product of their circumstances, and strive to understand their journey rather than judge them based on your own experiences.

MY FAITH JOURNEY AND LESSONS

I was raised in a household, where faith was not merely a Sunday affair but the very essence of our lives. My parents were strong-willed and deeply committed to their beliefs, and this devotion reverberated through our family. My father's parents were missionaries, roaming the country to support and uplift struggling churches. Their dedication to this calling set a precedent, and naturally, my father grew up in the church. He passed that legacy to my siblings and me, embedding the importance of faith into our lives from an early age.

The church was not just a place we attended; it was our home, a sanctuary where we gathered for worship and fellowship. I was baptized in that church, a rite of passage that marked the beginning of my spiritual journey. Over the years, I participated in countless activities—from Sunday school to youth groups, and eventually, I served as an usher. The pastor who baptized me also married my wife and me, and both of our children were welcomed into the faith through baptism in that same hallowed space. For the majority of my life, that church was my anchor; it was where I found community, purpose, and a sense of belonging.

However, as life unfolded—marriage, children, careers—I began to drift away from that consistent involvement. The once-frequent attendance dwindled. My wife and I became what some might call "Christmas and Easter Christians," only showing up for the major holidays. While we still attended church, we lacked the deeper engagement we once had. Life got busy, and our spiritual practices fell to the wayside. We didn't have Bible studies at home, nor did we read Scripture outside of Sunday services. Church attendance became more of a ritual than a meaningful practice.

Interestingly, my wife grew up in a pastor's family, so she had her own experiences with faith and church life. After years of being involved, we reached a point where we needed a break. We had the freedom to choose our involvement, and we chose to step back. I grappled with this absence of faith, often questioning why devout Christians seemed to face so many hardships. It was a struggle I shared with many, as we often turn to our faith during times of turmoil rather than in moments of joy. Why did it seem that the most faithful among us were also the ones who faced the greatest trials?

In my attempt to reconnect, I tried to immerse myself in the Bible. I listened to audio versions, tried reading through it, but I never managed to cover it from start to finish. Instead, over the years, I absorbed bits and pieces. I was familiar with verses and stories, yet I felt a disconnect, as if I were piecing together a puzzle without the guiding image on the box. After a long search, we stumbled upon a new church home that rekindled our commitment. My wife and I became active again; we volunteered, led Bible studies, and sought to integrate faith back into our daily lives.

However, life took us to Orange County, and the challenge arose: We loved our church, but it was an hour away. The long commute made it impractical to return each Sunday. We found ourselves in search of a new place to worship, eventually trying a small congregation. While we found the intimacy refreshing, the weight of responsibility was heavier than we anticipated. In a small church, every person's involvement matters profoundly; if someone can't show up or contribute, it can have a significant impact on the community. We found ourselves overwhelmed by the demands of that small church setting.

Ultimately, we ventured to Mariners, a mega church where we felt comfortable and engaged. We participated in a life group, connecting with others who shared our journey of faith. That group became a lifeline, a network of support, where we gathered monthly and cheered each other on through life's ups and downs. I realized that community is vital; it's not just about attending services but about being surrounded by people who uphold and encourage you. The friendships we formed there became a source of strength, reminding me of the importance of connection in faith.

As I reflect, I recognize how deeply intertwined my faith had become with every aspect of my life, including my business. I often share openly with others about how my beliefs drive my actions and my desire to serve the community. It became clear to me that without faith, I would struggle with anxiety and self-doubt, especially in leadership roles. When crises arose at work, instead of panicking, I found solace in prayer. My faith provided me with a foundation that calmed my fears and helped me navigate challenges with a sense of purpose.

Through pivotal moments, I learned that those who are faithful often face trials not because they are punished but because they have the resilience to endure. Their faith equips them to handle adversity, whereas those without such support may falter. This understanding reshaped my perception of faith and its role in overcoming life's obstacles. I began to see that life's challenges are not solely burdens but opportunities for growth and deeper reliance on my beliefs.

By 2022, I had transformed into a faith leader for my family, especially after the passing of my father-in-law, who had been a guiding light of faith in our lives. His absence was profound, yet it propelled me to step into the role he had once held, to ensure that our family remained anchored in faith. I realized I lived life now on a mission, a purpose bestowed upon me by God—a second chance to help others and share the gifts I had been given.

Forgiveness, however, has been the most challenging lesson on this journey. It is often the hardest part of faith to grasp, yet it has been the most transformative. I struggled with it for so long, wrestling with the weight of anger and resentment. But when I finally let go of that burden, my life changed. I found peace in the act of forgiveness, embracing it as a gift rather than a chore. I understood that no one is perfect, including me. If Jesus could forgive his killers in his final moments, how could I hold on to hate?

I want to be like Jesus—full of grace and compassion. Once I spoke the words, "I forgive you," and truly meant them, the hate slipped away, leaving me at complete peace.

In my reflections on religion, I've come to realize that faith cannot be forced. It's a deeply personal journey, one that each person must navigate on their own terms. Everyone's timing is different, and the desire to connect with God must come from within. It requires effort, perseverance, and an open heart.

This journey has taught me that faith can heal; it can lift burdens and transform lives. I've learned to surrender my worries to God, who keeps me grounded and provides wisdom in every challenge I face. My days are filled with gratitude, and I continue to learn from Him.

As I walk this path, I remain committed to my mission of helping others. The companies I manage are not simply mine; they are His. I am but a vessel, serving a higher purpose, and I embrace each day with the conviction that this is where I am meant to be. Many lessons I have learned in life are because of my faith and retelling these stories makes me realize how important faith has been in my life. So many of the stories about myself and others have been stories of faith. I now I can see it all in black and white.

Lessons Learned

- A supportive faith community can provide a sense of belonging and continuity throughout life's changes.
- Embracing forgiveness can lead to personal peace and transformation, helping to release negative emotions and foster compassion.

PART TWO

FAMILY, FRIENDS, AND FAITH

LOVE: WHAT DOES IT MEAN?

When it comes to love, I realize that I've developed a unique perspective over the years, one that has served me well in my relationships, particularly in conversations with my guy friends. There's a certain clarity that came to me when I began to articulate my thoughts on the different shades of love. It's a belief I've carried, often leading to deeper discussions and sometimes surprising revelations among those I care about.

When a friend confides in me about their feelings for their partner, they often struggle with this question: "How do I know if it's real love?" My response is usually straightforward, rooted in my own experiences and the profound bond I share with my wife, Roxanne. I've come to understand that love is not a singular emotion; it's a complex tapestry woven from different threads, each representing a unique relationship.

I've always believed that the love I feel for my wife is unlike the love I feel for my children, my parents, or my friends. Each bond has its own flavor and depth. For instance, the love I have for my kids is fierce and protective, a visceral instinct that I would lay down my life for them without a second thought. The love I share with my parents is rooted in gratitude and respect, shaped by years of sacrifice and nurturing. Then there's my love for Roxanne—my partner, my confidant, my forever person. It's a love that I would also give my life for, an unwavering commitment that has only deepened over our thirty-plus years together since we exchanged vows at the tender age of twenty-one.

To help my friends gauge their own feelings, I often ask them a probing question: "Would you die for them?" The hesitation that follows speaks volumes. If they pause, if uncertainty creeps into their response, I gently suggest that perhaps this isn't the love they seek. I've always known that if faced with a choice between my life and Roxanne's, I wouldn't think twice. I would choose her, just as I would choose my children without a moment's deliberation.

Yet, I find it intriguing how many people struggle with this question. They express doubt when it comes to their partners, and it leaves me pondering the nature of their relationships. Love, in my eyes, should be resolute and unwavering. If the answer isn't clear, it raises a flag—a signal that perhaps they haven't yet found their "forever" person.

Lessons Learned

- Each relationship we have—whether with a partner, child, parent, or friend—holds its own unique type of love. Acknowledging and understanding these differences can deepen our connections.
- Understanding your own feelings and defining what love means to you is crucial. It allows you to navigate relationships with clarity and purpose, ensuring you're truly aligned with your partner.

MEETING MY PARTNER IN LIFE

I met my wife Roxanne when I was just eighteen years old. It was one of those moments that felt like destiny. We were young, full of dreams, and perhaps a bit naive about what the future would hold. By the time I turned twenty-one, we were married, embarking on a journey that would shape our lives in ways we could never have imagined.

Our first child, Vanessa, came into my life when I was eighteen years old, followed by our second child, Grant, a few years later. Suddenly, Roxanne and I were young parents with two kids, trying to navigate the challenges of parenthood while I was building my business. From 1996 to 2005, I traveled extensively, making trips to central California (six hours away) every other week. Roxanne took on the monumental task of raising our children, managing the household, and ensuring our family was grounded.

While I was away building my career, I felt a strong urge to give back to our community. So, at age twenty-four, I started volunteering with a few nonprofits. Roxanne and the kids supported me in this endeavor, often accompanying me to events and activities. My wife was my rock, holding our family together while I chased my ambitions.

As the years went by, we faced our share of challenges. No marriage is perfect, and after two decades together, we encountered issues that tested our bond. But through it all, we realized we each had our roles and responsibilities. Open communication became our lifeline. We learned to talk about our feelings, frustrations, and dreams. It wasn't always easy; sometimes it felt like we were speaking different languages. But we were both willing to change and adapt, and this was essential for our growth as a couple. Roxanne and I worked through our struggles, emerging stronger and more united.

In 2017, after twenty-one years of raising our children, we found ourselves alone for the first time. Our kids had moved out, and the house felt strangely quiet. It was a big adjustment, but rather than drifting apart, we grew closer. It was a new beginning for us as empty nesters at age forty-two. We discovered new interests, shared more moments together, and learned to appreciate the quiet.

In 2020, I took a significant step and bought out my partners in my company, MVS. Roxanne was incredibly supportive during this transition. While she may not have seen herself as an entrepreneur like me, she became my voice of reason, helping me navigate the challenges that came with running the business. Her encouragement and insights were invaluable.

By 2023, I had bought the second business, and our dynamic shifted once again. Roxanne has also started volunteering for nonprofits, attending events with me for our foundation. It's amazing to see how our paths have intertwined, both in business and in our commitment to giving back to the community.

Looking back, I can see how far we've come. Through the years, we've built a life filled with love, challenges, and growth. Our journey has not always been easy, but every step has brought us closer together, and I wouldn't trade it for anything. Roxanne is not just my partner in life; she is my partner in purpose.

Lessons Learned

- Life is full of transitions, from young parenthood to empty nesters. Embracing change rather than fearing it can lead to new beginnings and deeper connections.
- A strong partnership involves mutual support for each other's ambitions. Encouraging and believing in one another can strengthen the bond and foster personal and professional growth.

OUR DAUGHTER, VANESSA

When I first met Roxanne, she had a three-month-old daughter, Vanessa. As our relationship blossomed, so did my connection with this sweet little girl, who was only six months old when my wife and I officially started dating. The biological father was absent, battling his own demons, leaving us to navigate the complex legal system in pursuit of full custody for my wife. Despite our efforts, the biological father would not relinquish his parental rights, leading to going to court to resolve.

In a decision that some may consider unconventional, we made the conscious choice to wait until she turned eighteen before pursuing the legal adoption process to make her my daughter. In the meantime, we chose to change her name at a young age, symbolizing the deep bond that had already formed between us. She embraced me as her father, and I embraced her as my daughter, creating a familial connection that transcended any legal paperwork.

As she approached legal adulthood at eighteen, we sat down with Vanessa to discuss the prospect of official adoption. With tears in her eyes, she looked at me and said, "Dad, I've always felt like your daughter. I want this to be official." The weight of her words hung in the air as we prepared for the legal process ahead.

On the day of the adoption hearing, the judge, a solemn

figure in his black robes, called me into his chambers. His voice was firm but kind as he explained the legal implications of the adoption. "She will have the right to your assets, she will be legally yours, and she will have certain legal rights," he said, looking at me intently. I met his gaze with unwavering conviction. "Yes, she is my daughter," I replied without hesitation.

In the courtroom, the atmosphere was charged with emotion as we stood before the judge to make our family official. The sound of applause filled the room as the gavel came down, sealing the legal bond between us. She was now my daughter in every sense of the word, and the weight of that truth settled comfortably in my heart.

This journey was not without precedent in my life. Adoptions had always been a natural part of my family's story. Roxanne had been adopted, and even my closest friend had experienced adoption. For me, the act of formally adopting my daughter was a continuation of a legacy of love and connection that transcends blood ties.

Despite maintaining some contact with her biological father's family, Vanessa ultimately found solace and security within our family unit. Her brief interaction with her biological father only solidified her understanding of where her true family and love resided. Now in her thirties, she works alongside me in my company, a tangible reminder of the enduring bond that transcends bloodlines and legalities. She has also blessed me with my son-in-law, Mark, and first grandchild, our precious granddaughter Delaney, thus completing our family circle with a new generation of love and connection.

Lessons Learned

- Family bonds can be created and strengthened through love and commitment, regardless of biological ties.
- Legal adoption can provide a sense of security and belonging for both the adoptive parent and the child.
- Patience and perseverance are essential when navigating complex legal processes, such as custody battles.

OUR SON, GRANT

In 2014, the course of my life was forever altered by a single revelation. Our son, Grant, at the tender age of fifteen, bravely told me and my wife that he was gay. As the words hung in the air, I could sense that this moment would mark a profound shift in Grant's journey, but little did I know just how profoundly it would impact my own.

Grant's announcement was a catalyst for a seismic awakening within me. It was as if a veil had been lifted, revealing a world vibrant with diversity and inclusion. I realized that, despite my travels and exposure to different cultures, I had failed to truly embrace the richness of the world around me. Grant, with his insatiable curiosity and open-mindedness, led me down a path of discovery that I had never before dared to tread.

His circle of friends, a harmonious blend of individuals from various backgrounds and walks of life, became an extension of our own family. They welcomed me with open arms, sharing their stories, traditions, and perspectives. Through Grant's eyes, I saw the beauty in their differences and the strength in their unity. I marveled at the tapestry of cultures that surrounded me, each thread contributing to the vibrant fabric of our shared existence.

Grant's authenticity and unwavering commitment to being true to himself has served as a beacon of inspiration for me.

He's challenged me to question my own beliefs and biases, urging me to confront my preconceptions and embrace the diversity that surrounded me. In him, I found a teacher, a guide, and a source of unending wisdom.

I am eternally grateful to Grant for being the catalyst of my transformation. He is not just my son but also my greatest teacher, showing me that it is never too late to learn, to grow, and to evolve. Through his courage and commitment to authenticity, he opened my eyes to a world of endless possibilities and boundless love.

Grant, with his unassuming presence and profound impact, forever changed the trajectory of my life. He is a gift, a blessing, and a beacon of light in the darkness, guiding me toward a deeper understanding of the world and my place within it. And for that, I will be forever grateful. Grant's courage and total dedication to embracing his true self inspires me to reflect on my own journey and the ways in which I could continue to grow and evolve.

As I watched Grant navigate the complexities of adolescence with grace and resilience, I couldn't help but marvel at the depth of his character and the strength of his convictions. His commitment to authenticity served as a powerful reminder of the importance of staying true to oneself in a world that often demands conformity.

In the wake of Grant's revelation, I found myself embarking on a journey of self-discovery and introspection. I began to question the beliefs and biases that had shaped my worldview, challenging myself to confront uncomfortable truths. Through Grant's eyes, I saw the beauty in differences and the richness that comes from embracing the unique perspectives of others.

Grant's impact on my life is profound and far-reaching, and his life serves as a guiding light in my own journey of self-discovery. And as I continue to walk this path of growth and evolution, I will forever be grateful for the gift of Grant's presence in my life.

Lessons Learned

- Embrace diversity and inclusion, as they enrich our lives and broaden our perspectives.
- Surround yourself with a diverse group of individuals who can inspire and challenge you.
- Remember the importance of acceptance, understanding, and empathy in fostering a more inclusive society.

MY MOTHER

The relationship I had with my mother has helped me recognize and appreciate the impact she had on my life. Amid the challenges, her tenacity and unwavering support were constants that shaped who I am today.

The numerous obstacles I faced—dyslexia, physical disabilities, and the challenges of wearing leg and back braces—made my childhood anything but easy. However, through it all, my mother emerged as my most steadfast advocate. When I was diagnosed with dyslexia, she didn't hesitate to step in and fight for my needs. I vividly remember her visiting the school, confronting educators, and demanding more comprehensive testing. "This isn't good enough; my child deserves better," she would assert with a fierce determination that left an impression on everyone involved.

Her involvement didn't stop at academics. When I faced back issues, she tirelessly accompanied me to numerous specialists, traveling to Children's Hospital in Los Angeles for consultations. I can still recall her relentless pursuit of answers and solutions. "We are going to find a way to make this better," she would say, her voice a mix of resolve and love. During my hospital stay, she was a constant presence, never leaving my side. She was there day and night, ensuring I received the best care possible, only leaving briefly to attend to her own needs.

In the months following my surgery, while my father returned to work, it was my mother who took on the role of caregiver. She was the one who helped me navigate the challenges of recovery, whether it was fetching me a drink or assisting me with daily tasks while I was confined in a body cast. Her nurturing spirit was evident, and I realized just how much she had sacrificed for my well-being.

Her intentions were always rooted in love and care. As I transitioned into adulthood and embarked on my entrepreneurial journey, I carried with me the lessons she instilled in me. She taught me the importance of resilience, the value of hard work, and the belief that I should never let my disabilities define my potential. “Don't let anyone tell you what you can't do; you are capable of achieving greatness,” she would often remind me.

Reflecting on my early years, I can confidently say that I wouldn't be the person I am today without my mother's influence. Her tenacity, caring nature, and relentless support taught me to strive for excellence and advocate for myself.

My mother was a champion of my dreams, and despite the challenges we faced, I am grateful for her unwavering dedication to my success.

Lessons Learned

- Having someone who champions your needs can make a significant difference in overcoming challenges.
- Acknowledging the complexities of personal relationships allows for growth and appreciation of the positives.

MENTOR: HAL KARLIN

As I sat in the softly lit dining room of the local social/business club in Orange County, the air filled with the rich aroma of gourmet dishes, a question arose that struck a chord deep within me. One of my colleagues turned to me, curiosity glimmering in his eyes, and inquired about my leadership style. "You know," he said, "everyone I meet in Orange County seems to know you. They talk about how outgoing, friendly, and happy you always are. How do you maintain that energy all the time?"

A smile crept across my face as I reflected on the man who had shaped my approach to leadership—Hal Karlin, our former CEO. "Well," I began, "that's because of my faith and lessons learned from Hal Karlin. He was the epitome of positivity, and I learned so much from him." Hal's story was a significant part of who I am today.

"Tell me more," my friend urged, leaning closer. "Who was he, and why does he matter?"

"Absolutely," I replied, feeling a wave of nostalgia wash over me.

Hal was the guiding force during my early years of my career at MVS. I had joined the company as an outside salesperson and after sixteen years of his mentorship, had ascended through the ranks to become president of his company. When he unexpectedly passed away in 2012, I found myself at the helm, entrusted with the day-to-day operations of the company he had nurtured.

Hal had always envisioned me as a potential owner, grooming me for leadership long before I ever donned the title. He had gifted me shares of the company, a gesture of trust that would forever resonate in my heart. In the final years of his life, Hal transitioned into a more advisory role, mentoring me as I navigated the complexities of our industry. During that time, I marveled at his unwavering demeanor—a tranquil lake amid life's turbulent storms.

In all my years working with him, I never heard Hal speak ill of anyone. His voice never wavered in anger; he remained calm, cool, and collected, treating every person he encountered with genuine respect. The man was a rarity, a treasure in a world often marred by negativity. I often joked with myself, wondering if he ever vented his frustrations privately after leaving the office. Did he bang his head against the steering wheel or unleash a silent scream? But outwardly, he was a paragon of kindness, embodying a steadfast resolve that seemed impervious to life's challenges.

Throughout our years together, we faced significant losses—ethically questionable employees, failures that could have rattled the strongest of leaders. Yet Hal never uttered a disparaging word. It was as though he had an innate ability to see the good in everyone, coaxing the best out of those around him simply through his presence. He navigated the complexities of business without ever exhibiting frustration or anger.

When Hal passed away suddenly after routine heart surgery, the world felt a little dimmer. I remember that Thanksgiving Day in 2012 when I received the heartbreaking call from his wife. The news hit me like a freight train, and I struggled to gather my thoughts as I prepared to inform the team of our collective loss. We all spent that long weekend grappling with the reality of his absence before returning to the office on Monday, a somber understanding hanging heavy in the air as this was the biggest loss in my life to that date.

Hal had been more than just a boss to me—he was a mentor and a friend. He had a daughter and often expressed how he had always wanted a son. In some ways, I felt as though I had filled that void for him; our bond ran far deeper than mere professional obligation.

Hal, an avid tennis player, had always changed into his tennis gear before leaving for the day. That Halloween, I had dressed as him, and when he emerged from the restroom in his tennis outfit, we shared a hearty laugh. The photo was framed proudly on his credenza, a testament to our camaraderie. Yet, when we searched for it as we cleaned out office, it was nowhere to be found.

Then, while helping his widow sift through boxes at their home, we opened a box to find that very photograph, along with other gifts I had given him. It struck me as deeply poignant that he had chosen to keep those items close, perhaps as a way to carry a piece of our relationship with him.

In our conversations leading up to his surgery, Hal had expressed a haunting premonition—he confided that he didn't think he would survive the operation. This revelation, coupled with the discovery of the items in the safe place at his home, added layers of depth to my understanding of him.

Hal lived his life guided by principles that echoed the teachings of compassion and kindness, even if he did not openly profess faith. He often told me, "If you believe in something and adhere to the values it teaches, you're bound to become a better person." His actions reflected that philosophy.

In the years since his passing, I have strived to emulate Hal's approach to leadership. I have never raised my voice in anger, nor have I belittled anyone in my charge. Just as he set an example through his actions, I aim to lead by example as well. My family can attest that I have never lost my temper at home either—and though they might recount a rare moment of frustration, it was never directed at them.

Hal's influence remains a guiding light in my life. It has been over a decade since he left this world, yet his lessons continue to shape who I am. His legacy lives on, reminding me that true leadership is not about authority but about kindness, resilience, and the ability to uplift those around you. In a world that often leans toward negativity, I strive to honor his memory by embodying the values he instilled in me, ensuring that his spirit continues to inspire and guide me every day along with his mindset of positivity.

Lessons Learned

- True leadership is demonstrated through actions rather than words. By embodying the values you wish to instill in others, you inspire them to follow suit, creating a culture of respect and positivity.
- Treating everyone with genuine kindness and respect, regardless of their position, fosters an environment where people feel valued and encouraged to bring out their best selves.

MENTOR: CHARLES ANTIS

In 2018, I had the pleasure of meeting Charles Antis, a moment that would significantly shape my journey in community service and philanthropy. Our paths first crossed at the annual meeting for the Ronald McDonald House Charities held in Los Angeles, where I represented the Inland Empire Board while he served on the Board for Orange County. The event drew board members from eight Ronald McDonald Houses and a camp across Southern California, creating a vibrant atmosphere filled with passionate individuals dedicated to making a difference in the lives of families facing serious health challenges at local hospitals.

As I stood before a crowd of several hundred board members, I shared my experiences from our capital campaign that had successfully raised $12 million to expand our house from twenty-three rooms to fifty-four. I spoke about the challenges we faced, the community support we garnered, and the collective effort that made our ambitious project possible. The energy in the room was palpable, and I could see Charles listening intently, his interest piqued. At that time, he was preparing to launch a similar capital campaign aimed at raising $14 million to double the size of the Orange County House. After my presentation, he approached me with a genuine interest in connecting and expressed a desire to learn from my experiences.

We exchanged contact information, and I started following him on LinkedIn. I was impressed by his commitment to community service and the various initiatives he supported. He was a man of action, constantly involved in efforts that uplifted those around him. Encouraged by what I saw, I reached out to him and suggested we schedule a call to discuss our mutual interests further.

When we finally connected over Zoom, I remember vividly that he was sitting in his truck, which was wrapped with the logo for his company, Antis Roofing and Waterproofing. It was a true reflection of his personal brand—bold and visible. We chatted about our work, and I expressed my admiration for his community efforts. I asked if he would consider mentoring me as I sought to leverage my business to help more people.

However, the call ended as he explained that he had a strict thirty-minute limit set by his team. I felt a bit puzzled and slightly discouraged, wondering if I had misread the situation. Despite this, I continued to follow him on LinkedIn, and we would occasionally bump into each other at various charity and business events over the next year. Each time we met, I was struck by his enthusiasm, and I could see how he effortlessly connected with others, bringing people together for a common cause of helping others with our resources.

In late 2019, Charles hosted an event at his office focusing on homelessness in Orange County, and I decided to attend. I felt it was an important issue that aligned with my values, and I wanted to learn more about how I could contribute. That event turned out to be a pivotal moment for us. As we spoke, Charles acknowledged my active involvement in various community initiatives. He remarked that I had been everywhere, doing everything he had been doing. It was a lighthearted acknowledgment, but it sparked a deeper conversation about collaboration. He suggested that we work together more closely and began introducing me to influential people in various nonprofits and the local businesses community.

Before long, our relationship evolved into a strong partnership. I jokingly told Charles that he never officially agreed to be my mentor, yet we began meeting several times a week to discuss our projects, share ideas, and brainstorm ways to maximize our impact. Our conversations turned from casual networking to deep discussions about our businesses and philanthropic efforts. At one point, he confided in me that I made him nervous, as I was doing everything he suggested, and he wondered if his philanthropic model would work for someone else the way it had for him.

I wanted to support his mission and be part of our shared vision for making a difference in the community. He seemed to appreciate my honesty, and it deepened the trust between us. As our friendship blossomed, we began confiding in each other about the unique struggles that come with being a business leader. Charles found it comforting to have someone who understood the weight of those responsibilities—issues that often remain unspoken in public.

By early 2024, after a few years of collaboration and friendship, Charles surprised me with an invitation to join the board of directors for his company. I felt honored but curious about his reasons for choosing me. He explained that he and his team wanted a succession plan in place, ensuring that their philanthropic mission would continue if anything happened to him. They had discussed various roles and decided that having a community leader and businessperson like me would help maintain the company's commitment to philanthropy.

Charles has become a cornerstone in my professional life as well as a cherished friend. Our shared experiences at events, whether charity functions or business gatherings, have solidified our connection. People have come to expect that if one of us shows up, the other isn't far behind. This strong camaraderie has not only enriched my life but also amplified our collective impact on the community. Charles Antis is not just a name in my story; he is a vital chapter that continues to unfold, shaping my path and inspiring me to reach for even greater heights in service to others. His "fearless giving" model does work and shows that others can make an impact like he has.

Lessons Learned

- Despite a rocky start with Charles, my determination to follow up and foster our connection ultimately led to a valuable partnership. Staying committed to building relationships can lead to rewarding outcomes. Persistence pays off!
- While I initially sought Charles as a mentor, our relationship evolved into a mutually beneficial partnership. Mentorship can be a two-way exchange where both parties grow and learn from each other.

MENTOR: JACK LONG

In 2014, destiny played a dramatic hand in the life of my friend Jack Long, a man whose name would soon resonate far beyond the modest confines of his Fontana neighborhood in California's Inland Empire. On an unassuming afternoon, he strolled into a grocery store, driven by a simple craving for a popsicle and the thrill of chance. With a quick pick in hand, he unknowingly set the stage for a transformation that would change his life forever—Jack won the California State Lottery, landing a staggering $63 million.

Suddenly, in a community marked by economic hardship and fading hopes, Jack became a beacon of light and wealth. His newfound fortune set him apart in stark contrast to the struggling lives around him. Yet remarkably, Jack chose to remain grounded. He continued to shop at Walmart, still picking up his three-pack of white T-shirts for $8.88 and the white socks that were a staple of his everyday life. The glint of wealth did little to alter the essence of who he was. He did purchase a minivan to accommodate his wheelchair, and he upgraded his mobility aid, but his lifestyle remained refreshingly unchanged.

Driven by a profound sense of purpose, Jack established a foundation dedicated to giving back to his community. He wanted to uplift those around him, and despite his wealth, he chose to stay rooted in Fontana. Over the seven years I knew him before his death in 2022, I had the privilege of serving on the board of directors for his foundation, witnessing the incredible impact of his generosity. Millions flowed from the foundation to support organizations dedicated to seniors, veterans, and children in need. Jack became a symbol of philanthropy, yet he detested the very term.

"I hate that word," he once confided, his voice tinged with palpable disdain. "Philanthropist—it feels like a label that implies obligation, a means of self-promotion. It's as if my giving is tainted by expectation." Despite his immense contributions, Jack craved anonymity. He sought no accolades, no spotlight; his only desire was to help those whose lives could be transformed by his generosity.

I once asked him why he believed he had been chosen to receive such a windfall and why he had chosen to give so much of it away. With a wry smile, he recounted a wild past, one intertwined with motorcycle gangs and a life lived on the edge. "God has an amazing sense of humor," he mused, reflecting on how the most unlikely person had been entrusted with such a fortune. "I can't buy my way to heaven, but I intend to leave this world a little better than I found it."

His perspective on philanthropy was both enlightening and challenging. While society often reduces it to mere monetary donations, Jack believed that true philanthropy encompassed a broader spectrum—an obligation to use one's resources, time, and talents to effect meaningful change. He made it clear that anyone could be a philanthropist, regardless of their financial situation, if they simply offered their time, skills, and connections to those in need.

Jack's disdain for the term *philanthropist* lingered in my mind, even as I found myself receiving an award for

Philanthropist of the Year in Orange County. His words echoed in my thoughts, prompting me to question whether the title was an honor or a burden. But then I remembered that philanthropy is not solely about money; it's about leveraging one's resources to make a difference. I strive to embody this philosophy in my work, using my business, my relationships, and my network to uplift those around me.

I am continually amazed by the extraordinary individuals who have graced my life. How many people can say they know a lottery winner? Yet, here was Jack, a man who had everything and yet chose to remain humble, inviting me to join him in his mission to make the world a better place. He valued my input, seeking my perspective on how best to allocate his resources. Together, we rallied to support worthy causes, creating a ripple effect of kindness and generosity that spread through our community.

In the end, Jack Long was not merely a philanthropist by society's narrow definition. He was a man of heart and action, a reminder that true giving transcends financial contributions. It lies in the willingness to extend oneself for the benefit of others, to forge connections, and to foster hope where it is most needed. His legacy inspires me every day to redefine what it means to give back—because philanthropy is ultimately about the impact we create and the lives we touch. Jack was proof that your mindset can change your life. He used his mind and heart to help others including me.

Lessons Learned

- True philanthropy transcends money. Philanthropy is not solely about financial contributions; it's about using your time, skills, and resources to make a meaningful impact in your community. Anyone can be a philanthropist by sharing their talents and connections.

- Wealth and success do not have to change who you are at your core. Like Jack, one can choose to remain humble and engaged with their community, prioritizing genuine connections over material possessions.
- The most impactful acts of kindness often happen outside the spotlight. True generosity is driven by a desire to help others without seeking recognition or praise.

MENTOR: DOUG FREEMAN

There's a gentleman in Orange County named Doug Freeman who has an inspiring story. He was known as one of the state's top attorneys for many years. Doug was also very philanthropic, though I don't have all the details of his backstory. At some point, Doug had a change of heart. Whether it was due to his experiences as an attorney or a personal choice, he decided to delve deeper into philanthropy.

In 1981, he had an idea to establish a National Philanthropy Day, a special day dedicated to recognizing those who give back to their communities. At that time, it was quite innovative—long before the idea of dedicating days to various causes became commonplace. Doug reached out to newly elected President Ronald Reagan, and through some perseverance—involving letters and a fortunate connection with a senior White House advisor—he connected with the president. He proposed the idea of having a specific day each year to honor individuals making significant contributions to their communities. It took five years, but he got congressional approval and President Reagan's signature on the bill on November 16, 1986, the first National Philanthropy Day.

Doug was invited to the White House for the proclamation, making the day a national event. The event is led by the Association of Fundraising Professionals, celebrated in

November across fifty states and two or more countries to recognize local heroes who are making a positive impact. It has been celebrated for nearly forty years, and it has grown into a significant honor. His influence has made the National Philanthropy Day in Orange County one of the largest in the country. People come from all over to hear him speak and to celebrate the achievements of local philanthropists. This year, they had more than 850 attendees at the event held at The Grove in Anaheim.

Doug, originally from Los Angeles, later moved to Orange County, where his former law practice still operates in Irvine. After retiring in 2007, Doug helped to launch First Foundation Bank, which went public a few years later. In 2017, Doug retired again and co-founded with Charlie Zhang the nonprofit Orange County Music and Dance, where he works as an unpaid full time CEO.

A couple of years ago, I was introduced to Doug by Charles Antis, who encouraged me to connect with him. I arranged a meeting at Doug's office at Orange County Music and Dance. The organization provides music and dance lessons to kids from five to eighteen years of age, regardless of their financial circumstances. When I met Doug, he was incredibly welcoming and knowledgeable about philanthropy in Orange County. He took the time to introduce me to others in the field and offered valuable advice.

What truly amazed me was his genuine interest in my children. I mentioned that my son was working for Steinway in New York and that my daughter owns a dance studio. Doug immediately wanted to meet them. I arranged for both kids and me to visit his nonprofit, where he spent an hour talking with them, asking about their backgrounds and aspirations, and offering his support. It was heartwarming to see him invest in their lives.

Over the past couple of years, I've attended the National Philanthropy Day luncheon, where many companies have been recognized for their contributions to the community. In 2024, MVS, Inc. was nominated for the business category award. We had six nominations submitted, and I was honored to be asked to join the judging committee to help decide who would win the awards.

When I learned we had been nominated, I contacted the chair of the committee, expressing my concern about potential conflicts since we were also nominated for an award. She assured me it was fine; I just wouldn't judge my category. I ended up judging a different category, and the process was fascinating. After each committee selected their top nominees, we all gathered to discuss and vote on the final recipients.

When it came time for my category, I had to step out of the room while they deliberated. I was nervous, knowing I would find out our fate upon returning. When I came back in, everyone was clapping, and I felt a wave of relief and excitement—our company had won!

We were honored with what is often referred to as the "Oscar Awards of Philanthropy" nationally. It's an incredible recognition that I never dreamed we would achieve, and the entire experience has been humbling and meaningful. Being on the judging committee also was a huge honor in itself.

Reflecting on this journey, I realize that what once felt unattainable became a reality. Through hard work, networking, and a clear focus on our mission, we're achieving something truly special. This award holds immense significance for me, not only because of its national recognition but also because of the wonderful connections I've made, especially with Doug Freeman. His humility and dedication to philanthropy have inspired me deeply, and I'm grateful for the experience and honor bestowed upon us.

Lessons Learned

- Engaging in philanthropy not only changes the lives of those being helped but also enriches the lives of those who contribute. One person's dedication can ignite a movement that uplifts entire communities.
- Embracing opportunities to contribute and engage with the community can lead to unexpected rewards and recognition. Taking an active role, whether through volunteering or participating in organizations, can open doors to fulfilling experiences and achievements.

MENTOR: JAY GOLDEN

Jay Golden, a masterful storytelling coach, dedicates his expertise to guiding CEOs on the art of narrative. Among his long-term clients was Charles Antis. One day, Charles turned to me with an intriguing suggestion. "You know," he said, leaning forward with enthusiasm, "you should consider getting a storytelling coach. I've got one who's fantastic. He could really help you articulate your story and elevate your business."

At that moment, I was struck by uncertainty. A storytelling coach? The concept was foreign to me, and I was skeptical. What would I possibly need such guidance for? Hesitant, I dismissed the idea, convinced that I could navigate my narrative journey alone.

Yet, fate had other plans. Jay decided to launch a unique initiative: a Storytellers Pod, a collective of CEOs eager to sharpen their storytelling and speaking skills. Rather than the more costly one-on-one coaching sessions, this format offered a more accessible group experience. For six months, I would gather with six other CEOs, each of us sharing our stories, critiquing one another, and learning together. Intrigued by the prospect of camaraderie and growth, I took the plunge and joined the group in 2022.

Over the next two years, I found myself rejoining the group, experiencing a rotating cast of CEOs while maintaining a steady bond with Charles. I wanted our original cohort, forged in the fires of collaborative storytelling, to remain connected, so I suggested meeting monthly for breakfast on Fridays. What began as a simple storytelling exercise evolved into a robust peer support network.

Each breakfast session, we'd gather around a table, sharing our triumphs and challenges, offering advice, and fostering a spirit of camaraderie. The essence of our meetings transcended mere storytelling; we became a lifeline for one another. When one member faced adversity—a negative community reaction to an event—our group sprang into action, providing counsel and organizing a special breakfast session dedicated to strategizing solutions.

This dynamic community became my inner circle, the trusted group I turned to for professional guidance and personal support. The accolades we achieved over the last two years—a testament to our collective efforts—were not solely mine; they were the results of the connections and encouragement I received from these remarkable individuals. It was they who championed my cause, nominating me for honors and introducing me to opportunities that I could never have accessed alone.

This experience has reshaped our identity, and now I share my story daily with newfound confidence.

As Jay says, the essence of this journey is storylistening—navigating life and communicating effectively by tuning into the everyday insights and narratives around us. We gather these stories and channel them into meaningful action through listening, collecting, and delivering on transformation.

Who is in your inner circle? Do you have a network of friends and business leaders who genuinely support you and want to see you succeed? Who pushes you to reach for more and strive to be better?

My incredible inner circle, the Storytellers group, includes:

- Charles Antis
- David Blair
- Julie Hudash
- Dawn S. Reese
- Ed Hart
- Jay Golden
- Debora Wondercheck
- Greg Hulsizer

Your inner circle is comprised of your closest friends or associates—a small, exclusive network pivotal to your journey. The remarkable people in my inner circle serve as my rock, both personally and in business, encouraging and building one another up, as stated in 1 Thessalonians 5:11.

Members of my inner circle have evolved into friends, business partners, and now board members. Sharing my "Forrest Gump" story at Jay's Legend OC event among other Storytellers was a defining moment that inspired the creation of new groups and encouraged others to share their stories.

Reflect on your own journey. Surround yourself with those who uplift and challenge you. Your story matters, and the right people can help you share it with the world. Let's keep building one another up!

The bonds I have forged through the Storytellers Pod have been instrumental in my success. Without these connections, I doubt I would have reached the same heights, as the weight of accomplishment often rests on a foundation of support, collaboration, and trust.

What I gained has extended far beyond business insights; I discovered friendships that blossomed from shared experiences. These individuals, once mere acquaintances, have transformed into genuine friends, sharing meals and laughter outside the confines of work. The leap of faith I initially hesitated to take has resulted in a vibrant network of support that has enriched my life both personally and professionally.

Lessons Learned

- Stepping out of one's comfort zone—taking risks and embracing new opportunities—can lead to unexpected rewards and friendships.
- Mastering storytelling not only enhances communication but also fosters deeper connections within both personal and professional spheres.

PART THREE

PURPOSE–WORK AND PHILANTHROPY

COVID-19 CHANGED EVERYTHING

Looking back on that unforgettable first day of serious COVID-19 brings back a rush of memories and emotions. It was a milestone moment for our companies as we had to quickly pivot and navigate through uncharted waters. The shutdown meant we had to triage the company and figure out how to keep moving forward. We were deemed essential, so our doors remained open throughout the entire pandemic. Leading the team through this uncertain time was a challenge, but we knew we had a responsibility to continue providing the necessary items for our customers.

The drive to the office during the shutdown was nothing short of surreal. The usually congested Southern California freeway was eerily empty, with only a handful of vehicles making their way through the desolate landscape. It felt like a scene from a dystopian movie, a stark reminder of the gravity of the situation we found ourselves in. Upon gathering the management team, the gravity of the situation dawned on us, and we knew that we had to come up with a contingency plan to ensure the seamless continuation of our operations. Our primary concern was ensuring that we had a steady supply of essential products to cater to our vulnerable customers, a task that proved to be a Herculean feat in the face of supply chain disruptions and shortages.

Amid the chaos and uncertainty, a glimmer of hope

emerged in the form of unity and solidarity among our customers. Despite being competitors in the business world, they banded together, extending a helping hand to one another and to us. It was a heartwarming display of community spirit and mutual support that transcended the boundaries of business rivalry. The sense of camaraderie and shared purpose that pervaded our customer base during those trying times was a testament to the power of human connection and resilience. Using my company, MVS, as the bond that ties them together, we helped move items from one home to another.

As we navigated the challenges of the pandemic, there were moments of triumph and moments of heartbreak. While we witnessed the unwavering loyalty and support of our customers, we also had to bid farewell to some of our most vulnerable clients who succumbed to the ravages of the virus. The loss was profound, a poignant reminder of the fragility of life and the stark realities of the pandemic. Our industry bore the brunt of the crisis, with each loss serving as a somber reminder of the stakes at hand.

Yet, through it all, we stood strong. We weathered the storm, emerging from the crucible of the pandemic stronger, more united, and more determined than ever before. The bonds forged in the crucible of adversity, the lessons learned in the crucible of uncertainty, and the experiences gained in the crucible of crisis will forever shape the way we approach our work and our relationships. The legacy of those two and a half years lives on in the resilience of our spirit, the depth of our compassion, and the unwavering commitment to serving our community with integrity and dedication.

Lessons Learned

- The need to pivot our operations and source essential products in the midst of supply chain disruptions emphasized the importance of adaptability and flexibility in the face of crisis.
- The unwavering loyalty and support from our customers during the pandemic showcased the value of building strong relationships and delivering exceptional service.

LINKEDIN, A JOURNEY OF SELF-DISCOVERY AND BRAND

I began using LinkedIn began as a way to connect with others in the business community in Orange County, a new area where I had no prior connections. It started with just one contact and no content, but it quickly grew into something much more impactful.

The first year, I did 365 days of LinkedIn—I posted daily for a year. It was a huge commitment and required consistent networking efforts, but my LinkedIn presence expanded to more than fifteen thousand followers and connections that year. This translated into real-life meetings I attended, including more than two hundred networking and charity events, leading to valuable relationships and opportunities.

The results of this investment in time and effort were undeniable. My companies received numerous awards and accolades, including being named Family Business of the Year from the *Orange County Business Journal* and being recognized as one of the top CEOs in the country by *Family Business Magazine*. These achievements were a testament to the power of building connections and giving back to the community.

Attending hundreds of networking and charity events in a single year was no small feat, but it was during these events that I truly saw the impact of the connections made on LinkedIn. Meeting people face-to-face, shaking hands, and having meaningful conversations solidified the relationships that had been formed online. Through these personal interactions, lasting friendships were made, business partnerships were formed, and opportunities for growth and collaboration emerged.

The connections made on LinkedIn not only helped to grow our brand and awareness in the community; they also led to some of my closest friendships. By reaching out, offering support, and meeting for coffee, I was able to establish meaningful relationships that went beyond just business.

In the end, using LinkedIn is about more than just networking—it's about building a community, supporting others, and reaping the rewards of those efforts. It's a reminder that what you put out into the world is what you get back, and that investing in connections can truly change the trajectory of your business and your life. LinkedIn may be the tool, but it is the connections made and the relationships formed that make all the difference.

Let me share my secret to success on LinkedIn and other social media platforms, resulting in so many honors in such a short time. First of all, I don't post asking for business from my connections. Instead I share open, honest, and authentic stories about my life, businesses, and nonprofits—both the good and the bad. I share my faith. I share what's on my heart. People do business with people because of their relationships. You have to get to know someone first, earn their trust, and then ask how you can help them. In return, 99 percent of the time they will want to help you and work together. I also don't follow all the so-called experts' advice on the correct way to follow the analytics. When I feel compelled to share something that I think will benefit others, I do. Everyone has their area of expertise and life lessons to share; what seems normal to you can impact someone else who doesn't have that experience. And sharing your time, talents, and treasures is a gift.

Lessons Learned

- Social media, such as LinkedIn, can be a powerful tool for building connections and establishing a brand presence in a new area or industry.
- Consistent and engaging posts on social media platforms can help to increase brand awareness and visibility, leading to potential business opportunities.
- Utilizing social media for networking purposes can lead to valuable relationships and partnerships that can benefit a new business.
- Social media provides a platform for showcasing expertise, sharing industry insights, and positioning oneself as a thought leader in a particular field.

THE MASTER'S PROGRAM—LIFE MASTERY

In 2023, I found myself at a crossroads. Despite the successes I had achieved in various aspects of my life and business, I felt an unsettling void—a lack of focus and purpose that began to weigh heavily on my spirit. Questions swirled in my mind: "Can my life really be different? Will I ever discover why I was put on this Earth?" It became clear that I needed something more—a deeper understanding of how to integrate my faith, work, and family life. That's when I decided to join The Master's Program, a three-year, faith-based course dedicated to life mastery.

This transformative course is designed to help individuals align their mind, body, soul, and spirit, guiding them from a mindset of success to one of significance. Bob Shank, the founder of the program, has dedicated more than twenty-five years to helping high-potential Christian leaders like myself explore and embrace their unique kingdom calling. His vision—to empower others to achieve a lifestyle of current success coupled with eternal significance—resonated deeply with me. It was this promise of clarity and purpose that drew me in.

Now, two years into this journey, I'm amazed at how the program has provided the focus I had been seeking. Every quarter, I engage in classes that challenge me to reflect on my beliefs and apply biblical principles to my daily life. In between sessions, I dive into assignments and readings that serve as both a personal and professional compass, helping me integrate my faith into my work and family life more seamlessly than ever before.

One of the most significant lessons I've learned is that it's not just about finding that singular "aha" moment, but rather equipping myself with the tools to consistently apply my faith across all areas of my life. This program has illuminated the path toward overcoming distractions that once derailed me. I've come to understand that my role as a visionary leader isn't just about day-to-day management; it's about creating a legacy that reflects my values.

As I interact with my classmates, many of whom are also navigating their own challenges, I've witnessed the power of community in fostering growth. We support one another, sharing insights that help us overcome personal obstacles. For example, when one of my classmates faced a significant personal crisis, he reached out to me even while grappling with his own struggles. It was a testament to the fearless love we have cultivated in this program—helping others even in our moments of vulnerability.

Ultimately, The Master's Program has provided me with a renewed sense of purpose and direction. It has transformed my understanding of how to weave my faith into the fabric of my life, business, and family. I've learned that life mastery is not just about individual success; it's about nurturing the connections that enrich our journeys and make us whole.

Lessons Learned

- The Master's Program has taught me how to blend my faith with my work and family life, creating a unified vision for my future.
- Life mastery is a journey, not a destination. I've learned the value of ongoing self-improvement and the importance of equipping myself with the right tools to navigate life's complexities.

FOUNDATION: THE WHY

The desire to give back to my community has always been a driving force in my life. In the early days, I was involved in various donations and served on nonprofit boards, but I felt the need for a more structured and impactful way to contribute. While my company already donated to nonprofits—supporting around 50 percent of our customer base—I knew I could do more to bridge the gap between my personal philanthropy and my business activities.

When I met Charles Antis, everything began to shift. As we worked together in the community, I found myself increasingly engaged with nonprofits reaching out to collaborate. This inspired me to delve deeper into how businesses can give back effectively. Charles introduced me to the concept of a donor-advise fund. I learned that with a donor-advise fund, a portion of company profits could be set aside to support nonprofits, providing tax benefits while allowing us to donate at our discretion.

After interviewing several organizations in Orange County, I decided to partner with the Orange County Community Foundation, a reputable entity known for its commitment to supporting families and businesses. In 2022, we established our fund, and over the following year, we proudly supported more than one hundred nonprofits. It was a rewarding experience, but I quickly realized that managing a foundation required more than just good intentions. It needed structure, oversight, and dedicated personnel to ensure its success.

That's when I met Crystal Cook, a talented individual who was working with one of the nonprofits I sponsored. When she decided to take a break from her career to focus on her young children, I saw an opportunity. I reached out to her with a proposition: Would she consider becoming the part-time director of our foundation? To my delight, she agreed, bringing her nonprofit experience and passion for community service to our team.

As we continued our work, we launched an annual Mental Health and Wellness Expo for C-suite executives, co-sponsored by our MVS foundation. The response was overwhelmingly positive, and many local businesses expressed interest in supporting our initiatives. However, we quickly hit a roadblock. The fund only allowed contributions from our own company, limiting our ability to expand our impact.

Recognizing this challenge, we made a pivotal decision in 2024 to transition from a fund to an official 501(c)(3) organization. This change opened the door for individuals and businesses to support our mission more freely. With the foundation now fiscally sponsored by another 501(c)(3) in Orange County, we were able to streamline financial management while laying the groundwork for our eventual independence.

Crystal has been instrumental in running the foundation, but I'm excited to pass the baton to my son, Grant, who is currently being trained to take over in 2025. This transition not only keeps our legacy within the family but also allows Grant to find his sense of purpose in helping others. I envision a future where my involvement in the foundation becomes my primary focus, ensuring that I continue to serve the community and address its needs long after I step back from the day-to-day operations of the business.

Ultimately, this foundation represents more than just a charitable endeavor; it's a commitment to using our resources—financial, physical, and human—to uplift those in need. It gives me a profound sense of purpose, one I hope to carry forward into the next chapter of my life.

Lessons Learned

- Establishing a formal foundation provides a more effective and sustainable way to give back to the community, allowing for greater impact and accountability.
- Transitioning leadership within the foundation ensures that the mission continues and that future generations remain invested in making a difference.

THE WEIGHT OF THE TOP HAT

Imposter syndrome (IS) is an insidious shadow that lurks in the minds of many, a feeling that gnaws at the edges of self-worth, convincing us that we are intellectual frauds. It whispers doubts that undermine our ability to embrace feedback, build resilience, and pursue success. At its most damaging, IS can deter individuals from applying for promotions, stunting diversity in leadership positions. To truly cultivate environments rich in diversity, equity, and inclusion, we must wrestle with this specter and reclaim our narratives.

Abraham Lincoln, born into the harsh realities of frontier life on February 12, 1809, embodied this struggle in many ways. His upbringing was marked by poverty. Raised in a log cabin in Kentucky, he was largely self-educated, with formal schooling culminating at the fourth grade. His education came from listening to the stories of adults who passed through his family's farm and from writing letters in the sand. Despite these humble beginnings, he would later receive honorary degrees, including a Doctor of Law from Columbia University in 1861, a testament to his undeniable intellect and perseverance.

Lincoln faced profound loss at age nine when his mother died. His father, grappling with land disputes, moved their family from Kentucky to Illinois, navigating through New

Jersey, Pennsylvania, and Virginia. Each transition molded Lincoln into a resilient figure, yet the scars of self-doubt lingered.

His journey into public service began in 1832 when he declared his candidacy for the Illinois House of Representatives. However, he momentarily set aside his ambitions to serve as a captain in the Illinois Militia during the Black Hawk War. Afterward, he tried his hand at various trades, from general store clerk to aspiring blacksmith, but destiny led him to a partnership in a New Salem general store instead. By age twenty-eight, he had opened his law firm, advocating for slaves' rights, and eventually ascended to the presidency during one of America's darkest chapters.

Lincoln's towering presence—physically and metaphorically—was accentuated by his iconic top hat. Standing at six-foot-four, the hat made him even more conspicuous in a crowd. He donned it through triumph and tragedy, in war and peace, and even on the night of his assassination. The battered appearance of his top hat reflected his frontier persona, embodying a man who didn't shy away from the weight of his responsibilities. Yet it was not just a fashion statement; it also served practical purposes, protecting him from the elements and storing important papers.

What captivates me most about Lincoln is not just his legendary life but what I read that he carried on him that fateful night in April 1865. Among other ordinary items, it's said he had a watch fob, a pocket knife, a white handkerchief, a single five-dollar bill—and in his top hat, eight newspaper clippings that praised his accomplishments. Why did he carry these clippings every day? Here was a man widely regarded as one of history's greatest leaders, yet he carried reminders of validation in his hat.

Even Abraham Lincoln grappled with the profound question that haunts us all: "Am I good enough?" This query is the nucleus of self-doubt for leaders at all levels. Lincoln's daily struggle with this question is a mirror reflecting my own insecurities, and perhaps those of many others who sometimes feel like imposters in their own life.

In our moments of doubt, our minds often succumb to confirmation bias, seeking evidence that reinforces our insecurities. To counter this, Lincoln built a body of evidence. By collecting newspaper clippings that celebrated his achievements, he established a tangible reminder of his worth. Each clipping acted as a bulwark against the tide of self-doubt, a daily affirmation that he was indeed good enough. And as a side note, who is on the five-dollar bill now? Lincoln! (At the time of his death, it was Alexander Hamilton.)

As I reflect on my journey, I realize that I, too, must construct my own body of evidence. This could be achievements at work, successful projects, or even kind words from colleagues. I keep a journal on my desk, a straightforward tool to collect and review these reminders. My evidence is not just a collection of accolades; it represents moments of growth, both personally and professionally.

Lessons Learned

- Gathering all my affirmations in one place makes them easy to access and review. I can see my growth visually, reinforcing the belief that I am enough.
- When doubt creeps in, I don't want to struggle to find my evidence. Keeping my journal close means I can easily remind myself of my abilities.

- Having tangible proof of my accomplishments solidifies their reality. This could be a folder filled with notes of praise, mementos from successful projects, or photos of significant moments in my career.

THE POWER TO CONTROL YOUR DESTINY WITH YOUR MIND

In what felt like a whirlwind, our company gathered for the annual strategic planning meeting. I found myself sitting at a large table, surrounded by key team members, as we prepared to map out our goals for the coming year. As I glanced around the room, I could see the familiar faces of my managers, each one ready to dive into the traditional template that had defined our past sessions.

"All right, team, let's get started!" I announced, trying to infuse a bit of energy into the room. The usual agenda unfolded: metrics, KPIs, and the same well-trodden path we had taken in previous meetings. Don't get me wrong; I believed in the process. I knew it was essential to set a vision, allocate responsibilities, and hold everyone accountable. Yet a nagging thought lingered in the back of my mind: We needed something more meaningful.

As we dove deeper into the meeting, I raised my hand. "I think it's time we revisit our mission, vision, and values. We've had the same statements for years, and while they serve a purpose, I can't help but feel they've become just words on a wall."

The facilitator nodded, encouraging me to continue. "What if we could distill our values down to something simple, something we could all remember?" I wanted our mission statement to be more than just a lengthy paragraph that no one could recite. I envisioned something concise—a statement that would resonate with everyone on the team.

Over the next few months, we worked on refining our statements. We crafted a mission statement that was a bit longer than I preferred, but it was what the team agreed upon. The vision statement was shorter, and I felt a spark of hope that we were moving in the right direction. However, I still sensed a disconnect; I worried we would hang these statements on the wall and quickly forget about them.

Then, through a board I was on, I met a father-son duo, the Portillos, who owned a business in a similar industry. They had a simple yet profound approach to their company values, condensed into just three words. When they shared their values with me, I was struck by their clarity. Three words, I thought. I can remember that!

Intrigued, I asked them how they arrived at those three words. "It wasn't easy," the father admitted, "but these words represent everything we stand for." I was inspired. I wanted that same clarity for my team.

Determined, I reached out to our vendors and customers, asking them, "What words come to mind when you think of Eric Goodman or my companies?" The responses poured in, and I gathered feedback from my team as well. We narrowed it down to three resonant words: Caring, Dependable, and Honest.

I made an announcement to my team during our next meeting, holding up a sheet of paper where I had written the words in bold. "These are our values."

At first, they seemed like just words—simple, even. But I made a promise to myself that these words would guide our actions and decisions. If someone was not caring, dependable, or honest, they wouldn't be a part of our team. Those values became our compass, and I made it my mission to embody them every single day.

I began posting our values on my LinkedIn page every day—a ritual that has continued without fail for the past three years. I incorporated them into our website and our communications. Whenever I faced a tough decision at work, whether it was about a vendor, a customer, or even an employee, I would ask myself, "Does this align with our values?"

"Eric, this is a tough call," I would think out loud, staring at the spreadsheet of potential vendors. "But if they're not dependable, it's a no-go. We can't compromise our values."

Some decisions were difficult, especially when it came to letting go of someone who didn't embody those principles. But I found that having these values to rely on made those tough choices easier. I could be honest and direct, explaining, "This doesn't align with our values of caring, dependable, and honest, and that's why we need to make a change."

As time went on, I embraced these three values wholeheartedly. They became more than just words; they transformed into our guiding light. I watched as my team started to embody these principles, too. They began to reflect on their actions and decisions, asking themselves, "Does this align with our values?"

I could see the difference in our interactions with customers and vendors. There was a newfound clarity in our communication, and it felt good to be operating from a place of integrity.

Whether you own a business or work for one, having

clearly defined personal and professional values is crucial. If your values align with the values of the organization, it creates a shared sense of purpose that propels everyone forward.

Lessons Learned

- Defining and embracing core values acts as a compass, helping guide actions and decisions and ensuring alignment in all areas of business and personal life.
- Gathering feedback from employees, customers, and vendors can provide valuable insights that shape an organization's values.
- Regularly communicating and embodying values reinforces their importance, fostering a culture of accountability and integrity.

MY JOURNEY WITH MVS

I began my journey with MVS, Inc (Mountain View Services) in 1996 as a consultant while simultaneously working at my family's company Chem-Pak. In fact, for two years, I balanced my full-time job with consulting as I focused on building a robust sales team and structuring their marketing efforts. It was an exciting time; I was deeply invested in both roles, shaping my skills while nurturing my passion for helping others.

In 1998, Hal, the CEO of MVS, approached me with a proposition: Would I help them hire and train salespeople to replicate my success? I agreed and began the process of onboarding new talent. However, the initial hires didn't pan out, leaving him frustrated. I had invested significant time and energy into training them, and their failure felt like a personal setback. It was a tough moment, but it revealed the challenges of cultivating talent in a growing organization.

Eventually, Hal suggested I join MVS full-time. I grappled with the decision. I had been a vital part of my family's business, serving as the vice president, and leaving that role felt daunting. I approached my dad, sharing the opportunity and my desire to explore this new path. He pondered for a moment and then said, "Maybe we can make this a win-win for both of us."

MVS was a significant customer of Chem-Pak, and my

father recognized that my departure could potentially benefit both businesses as MVS grew. Encouraged by his perspective, I decided to take the plunge, believing it would ultimately be advantageous for both companies. Little did I know, this decision would set the stage for nearly three decades at MVS and eventually owning it.

Over the years, I climbed the corporate ladder, transitioning from salesman to director of sales, then to vice president, and finally president. My original contract had been for one year, maybe two, but as I celebrate nearly twenty-nine years with the company, it's clear I found my place here. My aspirations had long included the dream of acquiring the company because I was passionate about our mission: providing care for developmentally disabled adults, children, and seniors. It felt like my calling because of my personal disabilities.

However, navigating a partnership with MVS's five other owners proved to be a challenge. Our founder, a visionary leader, was known for his disruptive ideas. While his creativity sparked innovation, it also required us to sift through countless suggestions and focus on what was realistically achievable. I became adept at filtering through those ideas, identifying which could be turned into actionable plans, but the strain of working with five partners was palpable.

Tragedy struck when we lost Hal, leaving just four partners. One partner eventually departed, reducing us to three. This shift created a power imbalance; with two partners against one, my voice became marginalized. I was driven by a vision focused on giving back and helping people, while the others prioritized scaling the business for profit. It was a clash of values that weighed heavily on me.

COVID-19 hit, further complicating our operations. The partners, who were older than me, expressed their exhaustion from the demands of the pandemic. They came to me and said they no longer wanted to work at such a relentless pace; they wanted to sell the business. They laid out their expectations for the sale, but I wasn't in a position, financially or otherwise, to meet their valuation. After listing the company for sale, we embarked on a grueling nine-month process of mergers and acquisitions.

During that time, I immersed myself in the intricacies of buying and selling businesses, collaborating with consultants, attorneys, and CPAs. The due diligence process was exhaustive, requiring extensive documentation and countless meetings about the company's financials, sales, and operations. I was simultaneously managing day-to-day operations while navigating the complexities of a sale during a pandemic, which added layers of stress as I dealt with employee absences and supply chain shortages.

As the nine-month process drew to a close, I felt a deep unease about the impending sale. I confided in my wife, expressing my concerns for our employees—some of whom had been with us for more than thirty years. I feared that the acquiring company, despite promising to keep things the same, might not honor our culture or the commitment we had built together. My gut instinct warned me that they might break the company into pieces for profit.

In a moment of introspection, I prayed for guidance and expressed my concerns to God. I hoped for a last-minute change, where the prospective buyer would back out, giving my partners and me a chance to renegotiate and keep the company whole. To my surprise, just days before we were to sign the sale paperwork, the company called, announcing they were backing out of the deal. It felt like a divine intervention.

I approached my partners with this unexpected development, suggesting we either re-list the company or that they consider selling it to me directly. They ultimately decided they preferred to sell to me. After negotiations, we struck a deal where they would finance the sale, allowing me to buy the business.

The entire experience, fraught with tension and uncertainty, reshaped my life and career. Though it felt like a tumultuous period, it ultimately paved the way for new opportunities. I learned invaluable lessons about mergers, acquisitions, and the intricate dynamics of partnership. Now I find myself at the helm of multiple companies.

Reflecting on that challenging journey, I see it now as a pivotal moment that taught me resilience and adaptability. While I initially viewed it as a negative experience, I have come to appreciate the growth it spurred in me. What once felt like an insurmountable obstacle has transformed into a foundation for future successes, my faith was always there to lead and guide me.

Lessons Learned

- When something doesn't feel right, it's crucial to listen to your gut. My instinct about the potential acquisition's impact on our employees prompted me to reconsider the sale, ultimately leading to a better outcome for the company.
- Preserving a company's culture is vital, especially during transitions. Maintaining open communication and

ensuring that employees understand the company's mission can help in keeping the team aligned and motivated.

FAMILY LEGACY AND THE COMPANY THAT STARTED IT

I knew for a few years my father was ready to retire from the business he founded and ran for more than three decades. He had discussed selling the business with me and had met with several companies regarding an acquisition. Given everything happening with my company, MVS, including our recent purchase and the challenges posed by COVID-19, I wasn't in a position to acquire his company. He ultimately decided to list the family business for sale. Although I didn't technically work for him, I had collaborated with his company as one of my vendors for almost thirty years. We had many conversations about the potential sale: Would a new owner continue our relationship with MVS? Would we retain our discounts? The implications of his sale could significantly impact my business, yet I felt unable to take on that responsibility.

In 2023, he approached me and said, "I'm turning seventy. I've run this business for thirty-seven years, and I'm tired. I want to retire." I asked about his options, and he told me he could either shut it down, liquidate the assets, or I could take it over. After discussing it, we decided to have the business appraised at fair market value. I bought it, which allowed us to keep it in the family and maintain our relationships intact. He agreed to stay on for a while in a consulting role to help with the transition. For the first six months, I didn't have to manage the day-to-day operations, as he was still there.

The entire process was emotionally charged. I struggled with the idea of my father selling something he built from the ground up to someone else when we could continue his legacy and potentially pass it down through generations. I shed a few tears and expressed my concerns to my wife about the future of the business.

Looking back, I believe my experiences have shaped my leadership style at MVS. Having started as an employee and worked my way up to CEO before buying the company, I have a deep understanding of what my team experiences. I worked alongside many of them for thirty years, which fosters a genuine compassion for both my business and my employees. In contrast, many CEOs at companies of our size often come from executive backgrounds and lack insight into the challenges their teams face. Thus, I believe my leadership style is distinctive because of my journey through the company.

Recently, I found myself engrossed in a television series centered around the men who run the Texas oil fields. In a memorable cameo, Jerry Jones, the famed owner of the Dallas Cowboys, shared a poignant moment with one of the characters, Hamm, who was in the hospital facing a serious illness. There he was, eyes glassy with tears and voice cracking, delivering a heartfelt monologue about how, a long time ago, he made the decision to work closely with his kids, and how that choice has made all the difference in his life. I love this idea of keeping family close and forging productive roles for them, blending business and family in a way that fosters connection and collaboration. It resonated with me, reminding me of the importance of nurturing relationships while pursuing our passions.

On the MVS side, my partners owned the building where the business operated. After I purchased the business in 2020, they informed me they planned to sell the building. Moving a distribution company is no small feat, especially with heavy equipment like refrigerators, freezers, and pallet racks. As I searched for a new location, I found that commercial real estate prices were soaring. Finding a suitable space would cost us significantly more than our current rent due to a special rate we enjoyed because of our ownership.

I went back to my partners to express my concerns about the significant costs and the tight timeframe for finding a new location. They informed me that the building was going on the market, and I would need to vacate once it sold. This created a challenging situation: I was making payments on the business while trying to secure a new building in a limited amount of time. One day, while driving home, I felt overwhelmed by anxiety about the business and the impending move. I pulled over, started to cry, and prayed to God for guidance. I needed my faith now more than ever. It had been a very hard few years with the pandemic and buying two companies.

Later that week, my father called and mentioned that his landlord had other properties and might be able to assist me. I set up a meeting with the landlord, Jim Franklin, whom I had never met before. I visited one of his buildings in Corona, but it was too small for our needs. I explained my urgent timeline and asked if he could help me find a suitable location. To my surprise, he offered to buy the building with me, assuring me he believed we were brought together for a reason. Though I was initially hesitant due to my recent business purchase, he insisted I call my partners and express interest in buying the building.

I contacted my partners, who agreed, and within a short time, my new partner wired the funds, allowing us to purchase the building. It was a surreal moment, especially since I later discovered he was a member of my church and had never crossed paths before this. The circumstances surrounding our partnership were remarkable, and my partners were pleased with the deal.

Ultimately, the entire experience, spanning two to three years, felt incredibly condensed, like it all transpired within just a few months. I bought two business and a building all on faith, and God provided.

Lessons Learned

- Change can be daunting, but it often leads to new opportunities and growth. Being open to change can lead to unexpected and positive outcomes.
- Transparent communication with family, partners, and employees is crucial during transitions. Open dialogue helps address concerns and fosters trust.

PERSONAL BRAND

While businesses like MVS and Chem-Pak have played significant roles in my life, they are ultimately just resources that support my true mission. My focus now is to cultivate my personal brand—Eric Goodman—where my faith, story, mindset, and beliefs take center stage. This shift is about more than just personal branding; it's about embracing who I am and recognizing that my identity extends far beyond the companies I have built.

Throughout the pages of this book, I have shared defining moments and experiences that have shaped me. However, I've come to understand that the essence of my story lies in my personal growth and the mindset that drives my actions. I believe that everyone should strive to develop their personal brand and identity outside their business. It's vital to discover your own narrative, align your mindset with your values, and lead with that authenticity. I want to be remembered not merely as "Eric from MVS or Chem-Pak" but as Eric Goodman—an individual who embodies determination and a commitment to personal growth through faith and mindset change.

Recently, during my reflections and prayers, I was struck by a revelation: I realized that I had allowed my businesses to become an idol in my life. In my pursuit of success, I unwittingly placed the business at the center of my existence, allowing it to define me and dictate my priorities. This realization has been eye-opening. The stories I've shared, the struggles I've faced, and the lessons I've learned all stem from a place where I mistakenly believed that my worth was tied to my business achievements.

Now, as I move forward, I am determined to shift that focus. I want my personal brand—centered around my faith and my identity—to be the foundation of everything I do. The businesses, the honors, and the connections I have cultivated will serve as resources that support my mission rather than define it. I envision my personal brand as a platform from which I can reach out to help nonprofits and support community initiatives, all while staying true to who I am.

This journey has taught me that it's essential to maintain a healthy balance and perspective. I encourage others to avoid allowing their businesses or external achievements to become idols. Instead, we should focus on building a strong personal identity that can withstand the challenges of life and business.

I hope to inspire my readers to reflect on their own journeys and consider how they can embrace their personal brand. The true essence of our lives is not found in our titles or the companies we build but in the values we uphold and the stories we create.

Lessons Learned

- Don't allow your business or external successes to define your worth or identity.
- Let your businesses and accomplishments support your mission, rather than becoming the center of your life.

MENTEE: ALEXANDRA

I often reflect on the journey of Alexandra and her success as a leader with MVS. When I first met her, I had no idea the impact she would have on my life and my organization. She was not just an employee; she became a pivotal part of our company's evolution, and in many ways, she taught me about my own biases and shortcomings.

The beginning of her story is a mix of humor and humility. I've always considered myself a keen judge of character, but I've learned the hard way that my instincts aren't always accurate. I have this tendency to form premature conclusions based on appearances, and it's a flaw I'm still working to overcome.

When Alexandra walked into the conference room for her interview, I couldn't shake my initial distraction. Her makeup was strikingly bold, with heavy eyeliner that seemed to draw attention in all the wrong ways. In that moment, I found myself wrestling with my judgments, all while trying to focus on her qualifications for the role of personal assistant. The latest makeup trends had taken over her look, and I was caught up in the aesthetics rather than the substance.

As I conducted the interview, I was aware that my focus was wavering. Instead of concentrating on her skills and capabilities, I was preoccupied with her appearance, thinking that her makeup might be a distraction. I left the interview feeling uncertain, sharing my hesitations with the manager who had referred her. "I was so distracted by her makeup that I couldn't really gauge her potential," I said, almost embarrassed by my own judgment.

Yet, despite my reservations, I made the decision to hire her, a choice that would ultimately prove to be one of the best I ever made. She dove headfirst into her responsibilities, demonstrating an unparalleled work ethic and an eagerness to learn. Her calm demeanor balanced my more frenetic energy, and we quickly developed a rhythm that made our partnership seamless.

About a month into her tenure, I noticed something: she had shifted her makeup style. I approached the manager again, curious if she had said anything about it. "No, I didn't say anything," she replied. I was surprised but relieved.

What truly amazed me was her initiative. Without any prompting, she began identifying areas of improvement across various departments. She'd walk into conversations with different teams, asking, "How can I help?" It was refreshing to see someone so willing to take charge without waiting for permission. She was not just my assistant; she was evolving into a leader in her own right.

As the years rolled on, Alexandra became a master of the business. She learned the ins and outs of every department. When I became president and CEO, I found myself without a vice president. It was time for Alexandra to step up. I approached her with the idea, and while she was initially hesitant, we agreed that for the first year, she would operate in that role without the title. She seamlessly managed the operations, allowing me to focus on the broader vision of the company.

However, the title was important for both her and the organization. I distinctly remember the day I insisted she put the announcement out. I sat in her office, determined not to leave until the memo was finalized. "You need this title, Alexandra," I said, explaining how it would empower her and clarify her authority to others. Reluctantly, she agreed, and that day marked a turning point for both of us.

After she was officially promoted, I saw a shift in her demeanor. Initially, she was apprehensive about how her peers would perceive her. "Things are going to change, aren't they?" she asked, a hint of worry in her voice. I assured her that it would be fine, and it was. She embraced her role with grace and confidence, proving to be an invaluable asset to the company.

Alexandra's journey wasn't without its challenges. There were moments of doubt, times when she felt overwhelmed and questioned whether she could handle the responsibilities that came with her title. I remember sitting across from her and reassuring her, "This is your organization. If you don't like the way it's running, change it." It was a simple yet profound realization for her, one that empowered her to take the reins and navigate her own path.

Over the years, I've watched her grow from a personal assistant to my right-hand woman. She has developed a deep understanding of the business, becoming someone who can run day-to-day operations without me. There's a unique comfort in knowing I can reach out to her, even on a Sunday, and find her at the office, diligently working on solutions.

Reflecting back on our journey, I realize how much I've learned from Alexandra. She not only proved me wrong about my initial judgments but also taught me the importance of seeing beyond the surface. One day, I shared my initial thoughts about her makeup with her. "You do realize," she joked, "that you almost didn't hire me because of my makeup?" Laughter erupted between us, a testament to how far we had come.

In the end, Alexandra's success story is a reminder that true leadership involves recognizing potential where it isn't immediately apparent and being willing to nurture that potential into something extraordinary. She exemplifies the notion that with the right support and encouragement, anyone can rise to greatness—even those who, like me, might have once judged them too quickly.

Lessons Learned

- Initial judgments based on appearance can cloud our perception of a person's true potential and capabilities.
- Providing support and encouragement can help individuals grow into leadership roles, allowing them to take ownership of their work.

BOARD SERVICE: GIVING BACK THROUGH TIME, TALENT, AND TREASURES

Throughout my nearly thirty years serving on several nonprofit boards, I've encountered a wide range of situations, but one experience stands out as particularly challenging and transformative. In that instance, I found myself in a position where I didn't feel valued and where my time was not being utilized effectively. It was a disheartening realization that I was perceived more as a funding source rather than a collaborative partner in the organization's mission. My desire has always been to work with nonprofits that genuinely appreciate and leverage my contributions.

Despite receiving offers often from other nonprofits to join their boards, in this position my talents were underappreciated. It was incredibly difficult to make the decision to resign from that board. I am not one to give up easily; I have always believed in the power of perseverance. However, I felt a strong urge to redirect my resources toward an organization that truly wanted and needed my support. The mission of the organization I was part of was indeed admirable, yet the leadership did not value my input or insights as I had hoped. This was a very prominent national organization—and it felt prestigious to be invited to serve on their board. Initially, I believed that my involvement would allow me to make a significant impact in the community. However, as time went on, I felt increasingly like my role was transactional. They seemed more interested in my financial contributions than in my insights or connections.

After much internal struggle and reflection, I realized that the organization was not utilizing my skills effectively. I tried to facilitate connections for the executive director, introducing her to people I believed could make a difference. However, there was a lack of follow-through, and my efforts felt wasted. I became increasingly aware that the individuals I had encouraged to donate were contributing because I asked them to, not necessarily because they were passionate about the cause. This realization weighed heavily on me, especially since the money I was donating could have made a greater impact elsewhere, particularly for smaller charities that could truly benefit from my support and engagement.

Ultimately, I decided to discuss my concerns with my wife and prayed for clarity. After significant contemplation, I made the difficult choice to resign from the board. It felt like giving up, and I wrestled with that feeling for a long time. However, deep down, I knew it was the right choice for both me and the organization. When I informed them of my resignation, they seemed surprisingly unfazed. It was as if my departure was expected. Shortly after, several other board members and key staff members also resigned, which confirmed that I wasn't alone in my concerns.

This experience taught me a valuable lesson: Even a great organization with a noble cause can falter if its leadership isn't aligned with your values. The mission might be admirable, but if the leader's vision and values do not resonate with yours, it becomes challenging to remain engaged. This prompted me to reevaluate my priorities and motivations. When I joined the board, I thought I was on the same page with the previous leader, but a change in leadership revealed a misalignment in values and vision.

Going forward, my advice to anyone considering board service is to ensure that you are passionate about the organization's cause and that you believe in the leader at the helm. If there's a disconnect, it's better to step away, even if it means sacrificing a prestigious title that looks good on a resume. Your time and talents are precious, and they should be invested in causes that resonate with your heart and mind.

After leaving that board, I joined two more boards, one of which was an honorary position due to a substantial donation of office space. Initially, I thought I wouldn't have time for board service, but I ended up falling in love with the organization and its leader. My involvement grew organically, and I became actively engaged in their mission. They even honored me by naming an award in my name—the Eric L. Goodman Philanthropy Award—which was both an immense honor and a testament to the positive impact I was able to make.

In stark contrast to my previous experience, I felt appreciated and valued in these new roles. The connections I made and the contributions I offered were genuinely utilized, reinforcing my belief that being aligned with the organization's mission and leadership is crucial. I learned that the right environment can not only enhance your contributions but can also enrich your life in ways you never anticipated.

These experiences reinforced my commitment to seek out organizations that truly value their members and their contributions. It has taught me that every situation, even the challenging ones, shapes my understanding of what I want and need from an organization and how I can best serve.

Lessons Learned

- Ensure that the organization's leadership aligns with your values and vision.
- It's okay to step away from a situation that doesn't serve you or the community effectively.

PHILANTHROPY: THE SPIRIT OF GIVING

The title of Orange County's Philanthropist of the Year for 2024 was not just a badge of honor for me, but a testament to the values and principles that have guided my business, MVS, Inc., from its inception. The word philanthropist is often associated with individuals who generously donate money to good causes. However, I firmly believe that philanthropy goes beyond monetary contributions—it encompasses the giving of one's time, talents, and resources to promote the welfare of others.

At MVS, Inc., we have always strived to use the resources we already have—our labor, trucks, buildings, products, and more—to make a positive impact in our community. We have opened our office space to nonprofit organizations, allowing them to use it as a base of operations. Our fleet of trucks is frequently utilized to pick up and drop off items for nonprofits in need. Our warehouse team lends their expertise to sort and store items, ensuring that they reach those who need them most. Additionally, we have fostered partnerships with our vendors, encouraging them to donate items to nonprofits in need too.

The value of these resources, if nonprofits were to pay for them, would be exorbitant. By donating what we have, we are able to alleviate some of the financial burdens on these organizations, allowing them to focus their resources on their core missions and initiatives. It's not just about giving money—it's about giving back in any way we can, utilizing our unique assets and capabilities to support those in need.

The guiding principle behind our philanthropic efforts is rooted in the belief that generosity begets generosity. Luke 6:38 reminds us, "Give, and it will be given to you," and we have seen firsthand the positive ripple effects of our actions. By giving back to our community, we have not only made a difference in the lives of others but have also inspired a spirit of giving in those around us.

The recognition as Orange County's Philanthropist of the Year serves as a reminder of the impact generosity and giving back can have on both individuals and communities. It is a testament to the power of using our resources for good, whether it be through donations, partnerships, or acts of service. By embodying the spirit of giving in all aspects of our lives, we have the power to create a more compassionate and supportive world for ourselves and those around us.

Lessons Learned

- Philanthropy is not limited to monetary donations; giving of one's time, talents, and resources can have a profound impact on others.
- Leveraging existing resources for the benefit of the community can alleviate financial burdens on nonprofits and support their essential work.
- The act of giving back not only benefits those in need but also inspires a culture of generosity and compassion in the community.

- By embodying the spirit of giving and using our resources for good, we have the power to create a more supportive and empathetic world for all.

RONALD MCDONALD HOUSE: PART OF WHO I AM

In 1999, my journey with the Ronald McDonald House began with the inception of a car show for the Inland Empire House. This event was not just about showcasing classic cars and motorcycles, but also about raising funds and support for the families and children who relied on the services provided by the Ronald McDonald House. Over the course of twenty years, this car show became a beloved tradition, raising more than $200,000 for the House and its mission of providing a home away from home for families in need.

Inspired by the impact of the car show and the mission of the Ronald McDonald House, I decided to deepen my involvement by joining their board of directors in 2003. This step marked the beginning of a long-standing commitment to the organization, culminating in my appointment as president of the House from 2006 to 2009. At just twenty-eight years old, I became the youngest president in the history of the Ronald McDonald House, a role that was both humbling and rewarding.

Over the years, I have continued to serve multiple terms on the board, with 2020 marking my twenty-first year of dedicated service to the Ronald McDonald House. In 2016, I had the privilege of being part of the Capital Campaign

Board, a pivotal moment in my involvement with the organization. Together, we successfully raised $12 million to expand the House, ensuring that even more families in need would have access to the support and care they deserved.

As time has passed, I have transitioned from being one of the younger members of the board to becoming one of the "older" board members. Reflecting on this journey, I am filled with a sense of gratitude and pride for the legacy I am a part of. The Ronald McDonald House has become more than just an organization to me—it's a part of who I am, shaping my values, priorities, and sense of purpose.

Lessons Learned

- Giving back to the community through initiatives like the car show can have a lasting and meaningful impact on those in need.
- Joining a board of directors or volunteering for a nonprofit organization allows for deeper involvement and support of their mission.
- Serving in leadership roles within an organization, such as becoming president of the Ronald McDonald House, can be a rewarding and fulfilling experience.
- Involvement in fundraising campaigns and capital projects can be instrumental in expanding the reach and impact of nonprofit organizations like the Ronald McDonald House.
- Long-term dedication and commitment to a cause can lead to a sense of fulfillment, legacy, and a profound connection to the organization's mission and values.

ORANGE COUNTY'S 125 MOST INFLUENTIAL PEOPLE

I was genuinely taken by surprise when I learned that I was named one of the Orange County Register's 125 most influential people. It's a county of over 3.2 million people. It was a complete shock to me! I started receiving text messages from friends and colleagues on a Sunday, and I discovered the news in the digital edition before it even hit print. As I read through the article, I noticed that I wasn't alone; there were other incredible individuals recognized for their philanthropic efforts. That filled me with pride, knowing that our community values the work being done to uplift others.

Reflecting on why I might have been recognized, I believe it stems from the impact of my contributions, particularly highlighted during National Philanthropy Day when we won an award. Being honored in front of 850 people at that event was a tremendous honor, and I never imagined I would be in this position. I've always approached my work not with the expectation of recognition, but simply out of a desire to help others. I was just doing what I felt called to do as my mission, and it's gratifying to see that the community is noticing those efforts.

However, with this recognition comes a certain weight. I've found myself grappling with questions about what it all means. "Why me? Do I deserve this? And if I do, what do I do with it?" These are the questions I wrestled with during my journaling sessions. It's important to me to embrace this recognition not as a pedestal but as a calling card—a way to amplify my mission.

The feedback I've received has been overwhelmingly positive. Many people expressed that they're not surprised by this recognition, given the work I've done over the past few years. But with those congratulations also come questions about the future. I've been diving into my faith and seeking reaffirmation about my path, wondering if I'm truly on the right track.

People have begun asking me what my plans are for the future, as if there's an expectation for continuous peaks of achievement. I've been reminded of the natural ebb and flow of life; after a high, there can often be a low. It's crucial to take time to rest and reflect, to allow space for vision and growth. I want to ensure that I'm not just chasing accolades but rather staying true to my mission of helping others.

This recognition provides me with a platform, and I feel a responsibility to use it wisely. I want to continue sharing my mission and encouraging others to find and fulfill theirs. I've made a list of people I want to connect with in the coming year—people who are eager to make a difference in our community. My goal is to reach out and ask how I can help them and what they need.

I came across a quote during my studies that resonated with me deeply: "Everybody wants to be king, but nobody wants to do the work of the king." It struck me how true that is—many aspire to positions of influence without understanding the commitment required to truly make a difference.

In the end, my mission remains clear: to help people and

uplift those around me. I'm grateful for the recognition, but more importantly, I'm committed to using this opportunity to continue the work I believe I'm meant to do. It's a journey of self-discovery and service, and I'm excited to see where it leads.

Lessons Learned

- Recognition can be validating, but it's essential to remain humble and focused on your mission rather than letting accolades inflate your ego.
- When given a platform, use it wisely. Leverage it to uplift others and foster community engagement. Your influence can inspire and empower those around you.

FAMILY BUSINESS OF THE YEAR HONOR

I never actually envisioned my company as a family business. For the first twenty-five years, I was the sole family member navigating the complexities of MVS. I had partners, and we collectively decided to keep our spouses out of the company—preserving our personal relationships while we built our professional lives. My children would occasionally lend a hand during summer breaks or after school, but I never truly considered that we were operating a family business.

I spent over two decades working alongside my father, but in a unique capacity—we ran separate companies. I was one of his customers, and he was one of my vendors. This arrangement worked beautifully; it allowed us to maintain our independence while benefiting from each other's expertise.

When I bought out my partners at MVS, something shifted in my perspective. I began to invite family members into the fold. My daughter, armed with a degree in marketing, became our marketing manager. My son joined the office staff, and soon after, my son-in-law came on board to assist with our e-commerce operations. Suddenly, my family was not just a support system; they were integral to the business.

Three years later, I acquired my father's company, Chem-Pak. He remained with us during the transition, guiding the sales department with his invaluable experience. It was then that the realization struck me—I now had my entire family working within the businesses. It was hard to deny that we were indeed a family business, yet I still viewed our companies as corporate entities filled with dedicated team members.

As I navigated the acquisition of Chem-Pak, I reached out to friends who had successfully taken over their family businesses. They generously shared their insights, including the structures and contracts that had facilitated their transitions. In one of our discussions, they posed a question that lingered in my mind: "You do realize that you're running a family business, right?" After mulling it over, I had to concede—they were correct. MVS was now a second-generation family business, and Chem-Pak represented a third-generation legacy.

Then came the exciting news—we were honored with the *Orange County Business Journal's* Family Business of the Year award. Although we had been in business for more than thirty-six years at the time, our presence in Orange County was relatively new, and I was thrilled yet realistic about our chances. I shared with my family and managers who joined me at the ceremony that we shouldn't expect to win, given the stiff competition.

As we sat among more than five hundred business leaders, listening to the nominees and their inspiring stories, I felt a sense of pride swell within me. When the announcer began describing a company that provided services for developmentally disabled adults and children, I thought to myself, That sounds familiar. My heart raced as I waited for the name to be revealed, and when it was announced—"Mountain View Services"—I was left utterly speechless.

Emotions cascaded over me like a wave; I was overwhelmed with gratitude and pride as I took the stage alongside my team to accept the award.

This moment was a culmination of years of hard work, resilience, and commitment to helping others. More than just an accolade, it was a reminder that our efforts to uplift those around us do not go unnoticed. Since that evening, I have wholeheartedly embraced the identity of running a family business. I've found a community of like-minded individuals—other family business owners—who support one another and strive for collective success.

Lessons Learned

- Recognize that family businesses are part of a larger community that supports and uplifts one another.
- Stay true to your values. Helping others quietly can lead to recognition; your good deeds will eventually shine through.

PART FOUR

PASSIONS–STORIES THAT DEFINE WHO I AM

THE JOURNEY OF A DREAM CAR: MY VOLKSWAGEN STORY

When I was a kid, my life revolved around Corvettes. Growing up, I didn't know a time when my parents didn't own one. My father was a true aficionado; at one point, he had a dozen parked in the driveway, each one a testament to his passion for these iconic cars. To me, every family must have a Corvette; it was simply the norm.

I remember my mom driving me to school in her Corvette. Those two-seater beauties meant I'd climb into the back, lying down in the hatch area as we zipped through town. It was unsafe by today's standards, but back then, it was just part of the adventure, and I thought I was the luckiest kid in the world. Corvettes continued to fill our lives through the eighties, nineties, and still today. My parents were heavily involved in the local Corvette Club, which boasted around 150 members, making it one of the largest in the western United States. My father even became the governor of the National Corvette Association, a role that allowed us to travel across the country for various events.

As I grew older, it was only natural that I would want to own a Corvette myself. I bought my first one, a 1985 model, when I was twenty-one. The deal with my wife was simple: if I got the Corvette, we could have a second child. So, she got the baby, and I got my car—a vibrant red beauty that took every ounce of our tight budget to acquire. I worked three jobs while she was in college to make it happen. It needed a lot of work, but I was determined to fix it up so we could enjoy it as a family at Corvette events.

By 1999, my involvement with the Corvette Club deepened, and I eventually became president. Under my leadership, the club flourished, reflecting my passion for these cars that had been a part of my life since childhood. But life has a way of steering us in unexpected directions.

Fast-forward to when my daughter was fifteen. She saw a little orange car for sale while on her school bus and called home, excitedly describing it to my wife and me. We drove to check it out, and it turned out to be a Volkswagen Thing. My initial thought was that it would be a great car for her since Volkswagens were known for being affordable to maintain. Little did I know, parts for these quirky vehicles were rare and hard to come by.

After purchasing the Thing as her sixteenth birthday gift, we embarked on a two-year restoration project. I quickly learned that finding parts was a challenge; I had to search all over the globe for what we needed, reaching out to suppliers in Germany and Brazil. The restoration process was a labor of love, and even though the car had no power steering or power brakes, it became a bonding experience between my daughter and me—just like in my younger years with my dad and Corvettes.

Despite our efforts, I ultimately decided that the Thing wouldn't be her daily driver; I was too concerned about its rarity and the potential for damage at school. Instead, we bought her a used New Beetle, and the Thing became my car. I fell in love with the Volkswagen culture—the community, the events, and the people.

Soon after, I sold my Corvette and bought a 1970 Volkswagen Bug for $650 on Craigslist. It was in terrible shape, infested with black widow spiders, and required extensive work. At the time, there was a growing trend of "rat rods"—cars that were customized with a rugged, unfinished look. I envisioned creating a unique vehicle that would combine the charm of a rat rod with beautiful design and craftsmanship.

As I gathered parts to bring my vision to life, I met an older gentleman named George at a Corvette Club meeting who had years of experience in fiberglass work. He agreed to help me build the car, and over the next five years, we dedicated countless hours to the project. We pushed the boundaries of what was considered possible, even installing a Porsche motor in that Volkswagen Bug.

After overcoming numerous obstacles five years later, we successfully completed the car, and I entered it into the prestigious Grand National Roadster Show. To my surprise, it won first place, marking the first time a Volkswagen had ever taken home such an honor for its class. The victory solidified our efforts and proved that with determination, anything could be achieved.

The car then embarked on a two-year tour, showcasing its unique design at car shows across the country and even earning features in several magazines internationally. The bond I forged with my friend George during this journey was invaluable, and I realized that the real treasure wasn't just the car itself but the relationships and experiences we shared along the way.

Eventually, I sold the car to a collector in Florida. Though I didn't recoup my financial investment, I felt satisfied knowing that I had brought my dream to life. I later received news that the car had won another big show, and while I haven't seen it since, the memories and friendships formed during that time will always hold a special place in my heart.

This experience taught me that pursuing your passion often means facing skepticism and challenges. If I had listened to everyone who told me it couldn't be done, I would have never experienced the joy of building that car. It stands as a testament to the power of perseverance, creativity, and the bonds we forge along the way.

That's my car story—one of passion, dedication, and ultimately, triumph. And while the road may twist and turn, the journey is always worth it. Again, my mindset was that I could do what I was told I could not.

Lessons Learned

- Sometimes life takes unexpected turns that lead us to new passions and experiences. Being open to change can uncover new opportunities and relationships that enrich our lives.
- Pursuing a passion often requires facing challenges and skepticism. The journey may be tough, but dedication and hard work can lead to remarkable achievements that defy expectations.

THE MICK

I didn't play a lot of competitive sports as a child, nor can I say I was a huge fan. My interests resided in a slightly different realm, one I poured my heart into with fervor: collecting baseball cards. There was something magical about flipping through those glossy cards, each one a tiny window into the world of the sport. I would spend hours at card shows all over Southern California, sifting through endless stacks of memorabilia in search of rare gems—mint condition cards and elusive autographs that seemed to whisper tales of legends long past.

Then, one day, lightning struck. We had a family friend named Dave Simpkins, a seasoned baseball collector and photographer, who was friends with none other than Yankee legend Mickey Mantle. Through Dave, my world expanded in ways I could hardly have imagined. I was no longer just a kid with a passion; I had the incredible opportunity to get to know "the Mick" himself. It was a dream for any young collector.

I remember the first time I met Mickey. It was during one of those summer afternoons when the sun glinted through the palm trees, casting playful shadows on the ground. Dave had invited me to Los Angeles to meet Mickey at a small charity event. I walked in, my heart racing, and there he was—a towering figure wrapped in warmth. Dressed in a comfortable blue polo shirt, his smile lit up the room, and suddenly, all those stories about him being this larger-than-life baseball hero felt real and accessible.

Mickey sat down with me, a young, starry-eyed collector armed with a notepad and a pen. "So, you like baseball cards, huh?" he asked, genuine curiosity twinkling in his eyes. In that moment, his stature diminished; he wasn't just a Hall of Famer, he was a kind man who took the time to recognize my passion. I couldn't believe it! I eagerly shared my collection with him, flipping through pages filled with legends like Garvey, Koufax, and Williams. Each card was a gripping story waiting to unfold, and Mickey listened intently, truly engaged.

Thanks to Dave, my humble collection suddenly began to transform into something extraordinary. He not only introduced me to Mickey but also helped me procure countless autographs from various baseball legends. Each signature became a badge of honor, a testament to my dedication and the friendships I had forged along the way. I remember eagerly waiting for packages in the mail, my heart racing as I opened them to reveal signed baseballs and cards that I had dreamt of owning.

Reflecting on those days, I can't help but recognize how fortunate I was to have such access to a baseball Hall of Famer. Mickey's kindness and generosity toward a kid with a dream left an indelible mark on my life. It was a lesson in humility and human connection: No matter how high you rise in life, kindness remains a fundamental ingredient for legacy. Mickey Mantle was a baseball legend, but to me, he was also a model of generosity and warmth that transcended the confines of the sport.

Even more so, it was Dave who opened those doors for

me—his passion for baseball and his willingness to champion a young collector helped ignite a fire in me that still burns bright today. Each signature, each card, and each moment spent meeting these legends taught me invaluable lessons not just about collecting but about life itself.

The joy I derived from putting together my collection went far beyond the cards themselves. It helped shape my outlook on interactions and friendships—all influenced by the kindness of men like Mickey and Dave. Both taught me that great things happen when you combine passion with genuine connection—a philosophy I carry with me to this day.

Lessons Learned

- No matter how successful you become, treating others with warmth and generosity fosters positive connections that can inspire and uplift those around you.
- The fulfillment derived from experiences and friendships often outweighs material gains, reinforcing the importance of building and maintaining meaningful connections throughout life's journey.

PHOTOGRAPHY—WHEN PASSION BECOMES PURPOSE

In 2017, my family and I made a life-changing decision; we relocated to Orange County. Leaving behind our hometowns felt exhilarating, a fresh start in a beautiful coastal setting. As Christmas 2018 approached, I found myself yearning for a new hobby—something that would allow me to soak in the stunning outdoor beauty that surrounded us. I had always admired breathtaking sunsets, and with my trusty smartphone camera, I had captured countless images over the years. It dawned on me: Why not invest in a proper camera and delve into photography?

After Christmas, I ventured to Costco and purchased a Canon camera kit. With excitement bubbling inside, I began venturing out to capture the picturesque landscapes of the beach. My daughter suggested I share my photos on Instagram, a platform I had never used before. So, I created an account and started posting my work. To my astonishment, I was soon contacted by a gallery in Los Angeles. They expressed interest in showcasing my photographs, prompting me to think, Wait, my work? I'm just a hobbyist!

Nonetheless, I submitted six pieces for their exhibition. My wife and family attended the gallery opening, where I sold a few of my images. The thrill of sharing my art with others ignited a passion I hadn't expected. When the Orange

County Fair rolled around, I entered some of my photos, and even though I didn't win, it felt rewarding just to be included.

Most of my photography focused on Newport Beach—especially the pier and sunsets. I found joy in capturing the vibrant colors of the sky as day turned to night. My passion deepened, and I soon learned that I had an addictive personality, always eager to learn and improve. I discovered that the Canon Factory Store in Costa Mesa offered free photography classes, and I eagerly signed up for a dozen sessions. For six months, I immersed myself in learning the craft, supplemented by countless YouTube tutorials. I quickly realized that while I had an eye for photography, I lacked the technical skills necessary to elevate my work.

As I honed my abilities, I began selling my artwork online, with my daughter assisting in creating a website. I was thrilled to sell dozens of pieces in various sizes. However, what began as a delightful hobby soon morphed into something more demanding. Friends and family began inviting me to take photos for them, and I felt pressured to continuously produce new content.

I poured significant resources into my craft, investing thousands of dollars in equipment. I found fulfillment in this pursuit, but it also began to feel like a job. Realizing that I wanted to give back, I decided to donate the proceeds from my artwork to charity. I partnered with an anti-street racing organization in Los Angeles, raising funds through auctions for various charitable events.

In an unexpected turn of events, I received a message through Instagram from Mariners Church in Irvine, where I was a member. They expressed interest in my photography for church events. Initially skeptical—my portfolio consisted solely of landscapes—I decided to explore this new opportunity. After connecting with their lead photographer, I learned how to capture indoor images and photograph people. Despite my nerves, I embraced the challenge.

COVID-19 hit, and suddenly, the number of photographers at the church dwindled. I stepped up and became the lead photographer, documenting every Sunday service for more than two years. This commitment meant sacrificing family trips and personal time, but I felt dedicated to the role. I was even asked to photograph the lead pastor, which felt surreal given my humble beginnings in photography.

Eventually, though, after two and a half years, I experienced burnout. The demands of the role weighed heavily on me, and I transitioned to photographing events less frequently. However, my journey didn't end there. I enrolled in Cornell University to earn a degree in photography, solidifying my newfound passion and skills.

By 2023, I had garnered recognition in various magazines, including House Beautiful, and my work was featured in galleries. What began as a simple desire to take photos turned into a remarkable journey of growth and achievement. My mindset was to learn how to master my skills.

Lessons Learned

- Sometimes, pursuing a new hobby can lead to unexpected opportunities and passions that enrich your life.
- Dedicate time and effort to learn the skills necessary to master your craft; this investment can pay off in ways you never imagined.
- While it's great to pursue what you love, be mindful of the balance between passion and obligation to avoid burnout.

WHAT FUELS A NAME AND WHY IT'S IMPORTANT

I found myself in a conversation with Jay Golden that changed everything regarding my vision.

I told him I had been struggling with our Mountain View Services brand. It was a name I had inherited when I purchased the company . . . but why did that name matter? Jay responded in a passionate and insightful way as a true friend who understood my journey. "You grew up in the mountains," he began, a twinkle in his eye as he leaned in closer. I nodded, recalling the days spent at the base of Big Bear, surrounded by towering giants that seemed to watch over me. "You took those mountains for granted, didn't you?" he continued.

I hesitated, then admitted, "I guess I did." We dove deeper into the metaphor of mountains and the business, exploring the connections that intertwined my life's narrative with that of MVS Inc. Jay asked about the origins of the company's name, and I explained that it was rooted in the street we once occupied—Mountain View Avenue.

"Was there a view of the mountains?" he probed.

"Yes," I replied. "They were right at the end of the street, colossal and majestic."

Then he pivoted, diving into the personal. "And what about your back surgery? Did you miss the mountains while you were stuck in bed?"

The question struck a chord, echoing in the cavern of my memory. "No," I admitted, "I didn't even see them for months. They were behind me, out of sight."

"Exactly," he said, his voice resonating with clarity. "Those mountains were taken from you when you needed them most. But now? Now you see them again, and your perspective has changed." With each word, Jay began to stitch together the threads of my life, intertwining them with the fabric of the business. As I reflected on the mountains, the challenges I faced, and the path I was forging with MVS Inc., I realized how deeply intertwined our journeys were. Just as I was reclaiming my view of the mountains, the company was evolving too, growing into something more significant than I had ever imagined.

Jay spoke of how as I transformed, so too did the company. "You're not just providing services for the disabled and seniors anymore," he said. "You're also giving back—to the community, to those who need it most." The metaphor of mountains loomed large in our conversation, symbolizing the aspirations we both held for the future.

Too many people take the mountains for granted, I mused. I had done so for years, not fully comprehending the beauty that surrounded me until it was obscured. Jay reminded me of how visitors would gaze in awe at the mountain ranges, marveling at the beauty we often overlooked. "That's the business, too," he said. "It's right in front of you, waiting for you to appreciate it, to expand it."

So yes, the mountains have always held a special place in my heart, not because I was an avid hiker or an athlete, but because they embody ideals and values that resonate deeply within me. Growing up in the inland valleys surrounded by them, I spent countless hours gazing at their majestic silhouettes from a distance, captivated by their grandeur and the sense of permanence they exuded. To me, they represented strength, stability, and the steadfastness required to navigate life's challenges.

In many ways, the mountains are a metaphor for my journey through life and my career. They stand tall against the horizon, reminding me that obstacles are often just part of the landscape. Life, much like the view from a mountain, can be breathtakingly beautiful, yet it is also filled with rugged terrain and unexpected turns. The mountains taught me that success is not just about reaching the summit; it's about the resilience to weather storms and the patience to wait for the right moment to ascend.

My company's name, MVS, serves as a constant reminder of this metaphorical relationship. It reflects my belief in building something enduring—something that, much like the mountains, can withstand the test of time. The challenges I have faced in my life and career mirror the ruggedness of those peaks. They require not just physical strength, but mental fortitude and a clear vision. Just as the mountains inspire a sense of awe and respect, I strive to create a legacy that commands the same admiration.

Ultimately, the mountains also symbolize my aspirations and the values I hold dear: integrity, perseverance, and a commitment to growth. They remind me that while I may not have climbed them physically, I can still draw strength and inspiration from their presence. I seek to emulate their enduring spirit in my life, embracing challenges with grace and finding beauty in the journey, regardless of the heights I may or may not achieve. The mountains are a testament to what is possible when we remain steadfast, and they will always guide me as I navigate my own path.

Lessons Learned

- Just as the view of mountains can change based on where you stand, so too can our perspectives on challenges and opportunities. Embracing new viewpoints can lead to greater appreciation for the journey and the potential within our endeavors.
- Life's obstacles are akin to rugged mountain terrain; they require resilience and patience to overcome. Success is not only about reaching the summit but also about navigating the struggles along the way with strength and determination.

CROSSROADS: TO CHANGE OR NOT

In 2020, I stood at a crossroads, a moment so pivotal that it felt as if the weight of the world rested on my shoulders. I had just bought out my partners, making me the sole owner of MVS. With the title came a gnawing urge to reshape the identity of the company, to breathe new life into a name I had never particularly liked. MVS—it seemed more like a placeholder than a true reflection of what we did. It was an awkward mouthful, a name that didn't tell our story.

I toyed with the idea of a rebranding, imagining how different names could capture our mission and values. Rather than dismiss his perspective outright, I decided to take a more democratic approach. We conducted a poll among our customers, vendors, and anyone else who had walked through our doors. To my surprise, the overwhelming majority wanted to keep the name.

So, I took a step back. Instead of a complete overhaul, we opted for a compromise: a new logo and a shorthand version of the name. Thus, Mountain View Services became MVS Inc. It was a small change that made a world of difference—an email address that no longer required a deep breath before typing, and a phone greeting that didn't feel like climbing a mountain.

I began to embrace my role as the custodian of this legacy. MVS Inc. was not just a company; it was a vessel for change, a means to help others and a way to illuminate the path forward. The mountains, once a backdrop to my life, became a powerful metaphor for growth, resilience, and the endless possibilities that lay ahead.

As I gazed out at the horizon, I felt a renewed sense of purpose. The mountains had been my silent companions through years of trial and triumph, and now, they were guiding me toward a future that promised not only success but a chance to make a difference. I was ready to climb higher, to embrace the view that awaited me, and to lead MVS Inc. into a new chapter—one where we would not only serve but also uplift those in need, reaching for the sky together.

Lessons Learned

- Engaging with your community—customers, employees, and stakeholders—can offer fresh perspectives and help you make informed decisions that resonate with those you serve.
- Personal experiences and challenges can serve as powerful metaphors that enhance your understanding of your business and its mission, helping you connect more deeply with your purpose.

WALKING INTO CLARITY

Walking is more than just a form of exercise for me; it's a ritual that shapes my day and my mindset. Like anything else in life, walking is a practice. It's a repetitive action that, when done consistently, transforms into a habit. Someone once told me that to learn something, you need to repeat it at least twenty times. When you do, it becomes second nature. This principle applies not just to walking but to every aspect of my life—from eating healthy foods to cultivating a positive mindset.

When I walk, I find clarity. The rhythm of my feet on the pavement allows my mind to wander freely, yet it also helps me focus. I often resolve work issues during these walks or reflect on family matters. It's a time for me to process thoughts without distraction. There's a profound connection between my physical movement and mental clarity. I've found that when I'm active, I'm less prone to the distractions that often cloud my mind.

In The Master's Program, I faced a unique challenge: reading assigned books. I've never been an avid reader and have often struggled to focus on the page. Then my instructor suggested an innovative solution: Why not listen to audiobooks while I walk? This idea was revolutionary for me. Combining the physical activity of walking with the mental engagement of listening to books transformed my approach to both reading and exercise. Over the course of a year, I read six books—an achievement I had never thought possible.

This fusion of movement and learning became a cornerstone of my daily routine. Walking not only fulfilled my physical exercise requirement but also opened my mind to new ideas. My instructor's mantra, "Leaders are readers," resonated deeply with me. It reinforced the idea that to be a good leader, one must be willing to learn and grow. As I walked, I embraced this mindset, committing myself to continuous learning and self-improvement.

My walking route around the Newport Back Bay is a sanctuary for me. The eleven-mile loop, surrounded by nature, offers a peaceful escape. The tranquility of the water and the beauty of the trails allow me to connect with the world around me. Occasionally, I pause to touch a tree or feel the sand beneath my feet, grounding myself in the present moment. These simple acts remind me of the importance of being in tune with nature, providing a sense of peace that is often hard to find in our fast-paced lives.

While I aim to zone out work-related thoughts during my walks, there are times when ideas and inspiration strike. Recently, I found myself pausing to jot down notes or send a quick message. Though I typically avoid distractions, I realized that sometimes, the best ideas come when I least expect them. Balancing work and mindfulness is an ongoing journey, but walking helps me navigate that path.

Walking is not just a physical activity; it's a catalyst for my mental and emotional well-being. It reminds me of the importance of routine and the power of a focused mind. Each step I take reinforces my commitment to growth, learning, and connection—both with myself and the world around me.

Lessons Learned

- Engaging in an activity such as walking consistently helps form positive habits that enrich daily life.
- Walking allows for free thought and problem-solving, making it an effective way to clear the mind and enhance mental clarity.

CYCLING AGAIN AFTER MANY YEARS OFF THE BIKE

The day I embarked on my first cycling journey in over a year, it felt like a triumphant return to a long-lost passion. The sweet morning air embraced me as I pedaled through the familiar streets, the rhythmic sound of my wheels spinning beneath me filling me with a sense of freedom and exhilaration.

As I navigated the winding paths and rolling hills, memories flooded back from a time when cycling was not just a hobby but a lifeline. Back in 2010, when I was diagnosed with my heart condition, it felt like my world was crumbling around me. The uncertainty, the fear, the relentless visits to the hospital—it was all too much to bear.

But in the midst of the darkness, a glimmer of hope emerged in the form of cycling. It was a revelation, a newfound passion that not only provided physical relief but also served as a mental escape from the chaos of my health struggles. The simple act of pedaling through the streets became a form of therapy, a way to quiet the anxious thoughts that plagued my mind.

I remember the first time I hopped on a bike after my diagnosis—the rush of wind against my face, the steady beat of my heart as I pushed myself to go further than I ever thought possible. It was a feeling of empowerment, of reclaiming control over my own body and my own destiny.

Over the years, cycling became more than just a form of

exercise. It became a lifestyle, a passion that consumed me in the best possible way. I delved into the world of cycling with fervor, devouring books, watching videos, and seeking out every opportunity to improve my skills and knowledge.

From my humble entry-level bike to the sleek racing machine that now graces my garage, each pedal stroke has been a testament to my determination and resilience. Cycling taught me the value of perseverance, of pushing through the pain and the doubt to emerge stronger on the other side.

And now, as I reflect on my journey back to the bike after a yearlong hiatus, I am reminded of the lessons that cycling has taught me. It's not just about the physical act of riding, but also the mental strength and fortitude that it instills. It's about embracing challenges, overcoming obstacles, and finding joy in the simple act of moving forward.

So as I basked in the glow of my long ride, I was filled with gratitude for the gift of cycling and the resilience it has cultivated within me. To me, it's not just a sport or a hobby—it's a way of life, a reminder that we are capable of so much more than we think. And as I look ahead to the miles that stretch out before me, I know that each turn of the pedal is not just a journey through the physical world, but a testament to the strength of the human spirit.

Lessons Learned

- Physical activity can have a positive impact on heart health.
- Finding a form of exercise that you enjoy can make it easier to stick with a routine.
- Mindset and determination are important factors in overcoming health challenges.

CONCLUSION: A JOURNEY TOGETHER

As I reach the end of this memoir, I want to take a moment to extend my heartfelt gratitude to you, the reader, for joining me on this journey. Your willingness to delve into my experiences, my struggles, and my triumphs means more to me than words can express. It is my hope that as you turned the pages, you found not just my story, but pieces of your own life reflected back at you.

Life is a tapestry woven from the threads of our experiences, and each of us has a unique story to tell. Throughout this memoir, I have shared my journey of faith, family, and philanthropy—three pillars that have shaped who I am and continue to guide me. I hope that as you read, you felt inspired to reflect on the values that are important to you and perhaps even encouraged to share your own narrative.

Faith has always been a cornerstone of my life. It has been my anchor in turbulent times and my guiding light in moments of uncertainty. I have learned that faith is not merely about religious beliefs; it is about trust—the trust that there is a higher purpose even when we cannot see it. I hope my journey has shown you the importance of cultivating a strong faith, whatever that may look like for you. Whether it's through prayer, meditation, or simply a quiet moment of reflection, I encourage you to find your own way to connect with the greater forces at play in your life.

Family is another vital aspect that I cherish deeply. The love and support of my family have provided me with the strength to face challenges and the motivation to strive for more. I've come to understand that family is not just defined by blood but also by the bonds we create with those who share our lives. I hope you've seen the significance of nurturing these relationships and the profound impact they can have on our journey. Cherish those you love, and don't hesitate to express your appreciation for them. Life is fleeting, and the time we have together is precious.

Philanthropy, the act of giving back to others, has been a fulfilling part of my life. It is through service that I have found purpose and connection to my community. I encourage you to consider how you can contribute to the world around you. Small acts of kindness can create ripples of change, and you never know how your efforts might inspire others. Whether it's volunteering your time, sharing your resources, or simply lending a listening ear to someone in need, every action counts. Together, we can create a more compassionate world.

As I reflect on the process of writing this memoir, I can honestly say it has been cathartic. Putting pen to paper, or fingers to keys, has allowed me to sift through my memories, to relive the moments that shaped me, and to articulate my thoughts and feelings in a way that brings clarity. I encourage you to consider writing your own story. It doesn't have to be for publication; it can simply be a personal exploration. Journaling or storytelling is a powerful tool for healing and self-discovery. In sharing our experiences, we not only honor our own journeys but also pave the way for others to find their voices.

I believe that everyone has a story worth telling. You may not think your experiences are significant, but I assure you, they are. Your triumphs, your struggles, your lessons learned—these are the threads that weave the fabric of humanity. By sharing your story, you can inspire others who may find themselves in similar circumstances. You never know who might be waiting to hear your words of wisdom, your hope, or your encouragement.

As I move forward, I remain committed to gathering stories—both my own and those of others. I will continue to work on behalf of those who need a voice, those who feel unheard or unseen. My mission is to inspire and motivate people to rise above their challenges, to find their purpose, and to make a difference in their communities. In all that I do, I aim to honor God and my family, striving to leave the world a little better than I found it.

I want to reiterate my gratitude to you for accompanying me on this journey. Your presence as a reader has made this experience all the more meaningful. I hope you carry the lessons from these pages into your own life. Embrace your faith, cherish your family, and find ways to give back. Share your story and encourage others to do the same. Together, we can create a tapestry of hope, resilience, and love—a legacy that will endure long after we are gone.

In closing, as you can see from the stories I have shared in this book, all the outcomes changed because of my mindset. I realized early on in my life—and later as a leader—that everyone around me reacted to my actions, which were decided by my mindset and my thoughts that controlled those actions.

I know I am not sharing a new concept or telling you

something you have never heard before. Much research has been done regarding mindset, and many leaders use mindset to help them. All the great CEOs, coaches, and professors share the importance of journaling, self-motivation, thinking positively, and manifesting your destiny. Growth mindset, positive mindset, faith mindset, health mindset—it's all true and works as you have read.

Mindset affects your willingness to learn and grow as a human and leader. I don't want someone with a fixed mindset on my team who is unwilling to improve, always thinking about failing and negative outcomes. I want team members with a growth mindset, those who are willing to learn, grow, change, and become better. They know they are going to make the outcome successful because they've already decided that.

Many Yale and Harvard Business School professors teach productivity and decision-making mindsets. Great leaders understand that personal growth and positivity are what makes a team successful. And it just takes one leader with the mindset to change everything.

Writing this memoir put it all in black and white, and I could see the role my mindset played on my life over the past fifty years. Weekly, someone will say to me, "How do you stay so positive? Do you ever get upset? Why don't you let things that happen in life bother you? Why are you are always smiling?" Now you know my secret—it's my Midwest upbringing and faith. I am living proof!

Thank you for being part of my journey. May you find inspiration in your own story, and may it propel you to make a positive impact in the world.

AFTERWORD

It takes courage to explore your life, especially in a time of great change.

Courage, from the French *couer*: "heart." It takes heart to recognize there may be more to the story than you've gathered, and to dive in.

In creating this book, Eric didn't stop at "life as it I've told it." What Eric discovered was that were many gems of insight that he had left by the side of the road. In traveling back through time and listening around, Eric explored many questions: What have I learned in this journey? What gifts have I not yet discovered? What insights have not yet been tended? What perspectives need updating? And what stories are relevant today to guide your audience to greater heights?

These are the questions I have watched Eric ask repeatedly as he has reviewed his life experiences, explored the meaning and relevance of his journeys, and worked to bring the meaning back to the world, to his work, and to his own perspective. Along with the other members of our CEO storytelling pod, I froze in my seat, drying my eyes, as I heard of the day of Eric's emergency operation; I felt the heaviness of his body cast on my own chest. My heart opened when I heard of his loving response to his son Grant's coming out. I celebrated his first "Forest Gump" story as he held those tiny orthopedic baby shoes.

It takes courage.

Eric didn't do this while lounging on a beach on sabbatical; he did it while running two businesses, commuting cross-county and sitting on many boards. And he did it because he was called to the work, in part because he witnessed Charles Antis stand in his own stories of purpose and presence.

I have seen the impact this process has had on him, and importantly, the impact it has had on those to whom he speaks. I've witnessed his willingness to give, to help, to join in causes.

And I'm here to say, though you know this now:

Eric Goodman is a living model of kind-hearted resilience in action.

You might not recognize the depth of this until you have learned his stories, but you sense it right away.

When I first learned of the dramatic challenges he faced in his youth, it changed how I saw him. Not just as an inspired, open hearted and wise-minded leader, but as a person who has overcome many things, through persistence, intelligence, and commitment to a better way.

As Eric knows well, when it comes to telling your story, there is no real afterword—there's only the next version! Because time keeps moving forward, we keep learning, and thus our perspective grows and changes. New audiences appear with new needs in a new time. And so the story shifts and grows; the takeaways emerge. It's a humbling act, this practice of life integration.

For a successful leader, it's especially hard, because the world has come to know you in one way, and yet you know that version of you can become like a cardboard cutout. People may be inspired by you; they may nod in approval at your insightful words and strategic moves. But deep down, you know there's more to it. And in the years I have known Eric, he has been nothing short of courageous in considering his insights, his lessons, his shortcomings, and his contradictions, all with the intent of being a better community member. His generosity in the telling has inspired many others to, well, get real with what they've learned and come through.

There's a greater gift to the process: Your updated stories update your operating system. It gets you to see differently through a new lens, through the perspective of today.

One moment with Eric sticks out in memory. As he mentioned in his story about our CEO storyteller pod, Eric decided that he had to stay connected with our group through a monthly breakfast. As I live in Oregon, I often wouldn't be able to attend these sessions. But every month, I'd hear about the conversations that were happening, the collaborations that were being spawned, and most of all, the "being real." I'd hear from one member or another about some real talk about financial challenges, health challenges, family challenges, and I'd watch through our text string how honest we had all become with one another.

I believe that this elevated level of trust was built through the vulnerability and mutual support that came through our story-sharing and our story-listening. But it only was able to really blossom because Eric brought that extra insight: "We have to keep this going!" It's that enthusiasm, that living energy, that willingness to study life as it comes, that makes Eric a very special person.

It's not just the awards he's received over the past few years for his contributions. It's that he himself is the contribution—Eric Goodman, the good-man that is Eric. His devotion elevates the good around us; and my sense is he is only just getting started.

—Jay Golden
CEO, Chief Storyteller, Retellable

ABOUT THE AUTHOR

Eric L. Goodman is a respected community leader, author, speaker, philanthropist, and the owner and CEO of multiple companies based in Southern California.

Eric fosters his core belief in building relationships within the community. He has served on the board of directors for several prominent nonprofit organizations, including the American Heart Association and Ronald McDonald House Charities, Mountain Shadows Foundation, CSUF Center for Leadership, Passkeys Foundation, Junior Achievement, Team Kids and Orange County Department of Education: Bright Futures Foundation. Along with many nonprofit committees and advisory boards.

Eric has been married to his wife, Roxanne, for more than thirty years. They have two children, Vanessa and Grant, a son-in-law, Mark, and one grandchild, Delaney.

Eric holds a passion for photography. His work has appeared in galleries, and all proceeds from his work are donated to charity. Eric holds a degree in photography from Cornell University.

Eric is also a classic car enthusiast. He is President of the Vintage Volkswagen Club of America, the largest Vintage Volkswagen club in the county. He has served on the board since 2018.

Honors

Points of Light, the Civic 50 Award honoree in 2022, 2023, and 2024, being recognized as one of the top 50 most community-minded companies in Orange County

The Unforgettables Foundations, Heart of the Inland Empire Award 2020

OneOC's, Spirit of Volunteerism Award honoree 2022-2025

CSUSB Center for Entrepreneurships Spirit of the Entrepreneur Award Finalist 2022

CSUF Center for Leaderships, Leadership Excellence in Community Engagement Award 2023

The Orange County Business Journal's Medium-Sized Family-Owned Business of the Year 2023.

Family Business Magazine's Top CEO 2023.

Institute for Community Impacts, Pillar of the Community in Business Award 2023

Orange County Business Journal's OC 500 list of influential and notable individuals in Orange County

Junior Achievement, JA Inspire Award 2023

CSUF Center for Family Business Family Business, Hall of Fame Finalist 2023

Orange County Business Journal's Excellence in Entrepreneurship Awards Finalist 2024

Associate of Corporate Growth, Orange County's Corporate Responsibility Award 2024

Greater Irvine Chamber, Philanthropist of the Year in 2024

Association of Fundraising Professionals, Orange County National Philanthropy Day, Outstanding Small Business of the Year 2024

Orange Country Register's 125 Most Influential People in Orange County for 2024

JPMoganChase, ICONS Awards Finalist 2024

Junior Achievement, Eric L. Goodman Philanthropy Impact Award 2024

Triple-S, Presidents Award 2025

MY FAVORITE SAYINGS

Almighty God—Faith to believe, Grace to save and Works to glorify.

Leaders are readers.

Growth is a process not a miracle.

Dream it, plan it, do it.

Career versus calling—create time to serve.

Lead by example.

Grace: what he did for me.

Happiness is a state of mind.

Get trust, give trust.

No excuses, only solutions.

In a world where you can be anything, be yourself.

Success is the best revenge.

MINDSET QUOTES

Courage is not the absence of fear, but the willingness to face it head on.

Never underestimate the power of determination and perseverance.

Don't let the opinions of others define who you are and what you can achieve.

Never compromise your values for the sake of fitting in or pleasing others.

Failure is simply a stepping stone toward success.

Always strive to be the best version of yourself, no matter the circumstances.

The greatest battles in life are fought within ourselves.

Success is not measured by material possessions but by the impact you have on others.

Never underestimate the power of kindness and compassion.

Success is not an overnight phenomenon; it is the result of years of hard work and determination.

Don't let past failures define your future success.

Forgiveness is not a sign of weakness, but a display of strength.

The only limitations in life are the ones you impose on yourself.

Never stop learning and growing, no matter how old you are.

Every setback is an opportunity to come back stronger than ever.

Never underestimate the power of a determined mind.

The key to true success is to never stop learning and growing.

Success is not about how much you have, but how much you give.

The greatest reward in life is knowing that you've made a positive impact on someone else's life.